Faithful and Clear

A Pastor's Guide to Church Governance: Constitutions, Bylaws, Policies, and Procedures

Brad Gwartney

Faithful and Clear

A Pastor's Guide to Church Governance: Constitutions, Bylaws, Policies, and Procedures

Copyright © 2026 by Brad Gwartney

All rights reserved. No part of this publication may be reproduced, stored in a retrieval system, or transmitted in any form or by any means—electronic, mechanical, photocopy, recording, or otherwise—without prior written permission of the author, except for brief quotations in reviews or articles.

Unless otherwise noted, Scripture quotations are from the Holy Bible, English Standard Version (ESV).

This book is intended for educational and informational purposes only. It is not intended to provide legal, financial, or professional advice. Readers should consult appropriate professionals for guidance related to their specific situation. While every effort has been made to ensure accuracy, the author assumes no responsibility for errors or omissions or for the results obtained from the use of this information.

The examples and scenarios included in this book are provided for illustrative purposes only.

Independently published

www.bradgwartney.com

ISBN: 979-8-234-08413-2

First Edition

To my wife, June. Thank you for your love, patience, and encouragement to finish this work. I could not have done it without you.

To Lydia and Will. Thank you for putting up with all the extra hours this project took and for cheering me on along the way. I love you both and am proud to be your dad.

And to my parents, Tim and Vicki Gwartney. Thank you for your faithful example, your love for the Lord, and the foundation you helped build in my life and ministry.

ACKNOWLEDGMENTS

This book grew out of a journey that has been both academic and deeply practical.

I first began studying church governance more systematically through my doctoral work at New Orleans Baptist Theological Seminary. I am grateful to the faculty at NOBTS who challenged me to think carefully, write clearly, and serve the church faithfully. I am especially thankful to my advisor, Dr. Jody Dean, who helped me complete my Doctor of Ministry degree and encouraged me to develop the work from that project into a resource for pastors and churches. This book is my humble attempt to honor that commitment.

Much of what I have learned about church governance, however, was not learned only in a classroom. It was learned in the real-life context of local church ministry. I am thankful for the pastors, leaders, and members of the churches I have served, who allowed me to learn, grow, make mistakes, and keep trying to help the church make a difference in its community.

I am grateful to Dr. Mike Keown and the people of First Newark Baptist Church in Thomasville, Georgia, where I learned important lessons in ministry, leadership, and faithfulness. I was young, still learning, and given the grace to grow through mistakes.

I am thankful to Matt Hall and Canopy Roads Baptist Church in Tallahassee, where I continued to deepen my understanding of how church systems can either support or complicate ministry. During that season, I also learned more about denominational leadership and what it means to truly love and serve the church.

I am especially grateful for Dr. Dan Glenn and Stetson Baptist Church in DeLand, Florida, where I currently serve. Stetson has provided a place to lead, learn, and practice many of the principles discussed in this book. The pastors, staff, leaders, and members of Stetson Baptist Church have influenced my understanding of governance, ministry, and what it truly means to serve the church with faithfulness and clarity.

To every church member, pastor, staff member, professor, denominational leader, lay leader, and friend who has been part of this journey, thank you. This book reflects lessons learned alongside you, often through trial and error, and always with the desire to strengthen the local church for the mission God has given it.

INTRODUCTION

A passion for church governance rarely draws someone into ministry. Most pastors feel called to preach God's Word, shepherd people, and lead the church in its mission. Few begin ministry with a desire to write bylaws, develop policies, or manage organizational details. As a result, governance is often set aside for later, when there is more time or when a problem makes it unavoidable. Yet it is important to recognize that guiding a church through governance is itself a vital ministry calling. Faithful governance work cares for the flock and upholds the church's witness, and those who serve in this area help create an environment where gospel ministry can flourish. This encouragement is for those who may feel unqualified or reluctant: your governance work is a genuine act of service to Christ and his church.

This resource is not intended to turn pastors into lawyers or to make churches feel more corporate. Its purpose is simpler: to help churches establish **FAITHFUL, CLEAR** governance structures that support ministry rather than hinder it.

Those two words matter.

Governance should be faithful because the church belongs to Christ. The structures that guide a church's life together should reflect Scripture, support the Great Commission, and help leaders steward God's people with care. In Acts 6:1–7, the early church addressed organizational needs by appointing leaders to serve, demonstrating the importance of faithful structures in supporting ministry. Similarly, 1 Timothy 3 outlines qualifications for church leaders, grounding governance in biblical authority. Governance should never become an end in itself. It should serve the mission of the church and help the congregation live together in a way that honors the Lord.

Governance should also be clear because confusion places unnecessary burdens on leaders and members. When authority is vague, expectations are assumed, and processes are inconsistent, trust begins to erode. Clear governance helps people understand how decisions are made, who is responsible, and how the church moves forward together.

Faithful governance keeps the church anchored in its mission. Clear governance helps the church live out that mission with trust and unity.

Each chapter examines key elements of church governance, including constitutions, bylaws, policies, and procedures, and analyzes how these structures function in real churches facing real challenges. Throughout the book, you will find case studies that illustrate both the successes and struggles churches have faced as they worked to clarify governance and lead well. These examples are included to help leaders see how the principles discussed can be applied in practical, relatable situations. Rather than increasing complexity or rigidity, the intent is to clarify processes and promote stability. Rather than instilling fear, the aim is to support faithfulness.

Many churches begin governance discussions out of concern for worst-case scenarios. While preparing for those moments is wise, governance is not only about responding to problems. It is about shaping how the church reflects God's character in everyday decisions. How a church handles authority, communicates expectations, and resolves conflict all communicate its values and its witness.

Because of this, governance is not just administrative. It is pastoral.

Church leaders are responsible for examining every aspect of the church's life and ensuring it reflects God's character and supports the Great Commission. Governance structures are one way this responsibility is carried out. When those structures are clear and aligned, they create an environment in which leaders can lead effectively, members can trust the process, and the church can move forward in unity.

This book is written for pastors, staff, lay leaders, and future ministry leaders who want to strengthen the foundation of their church's governance. Some readers may be leading revitalization efforts. Others may be seeking to clarify existing structures, prepare for future growth, or better understand the role governance plays in faithful church leadership. Wherever a church may be, the goal remains the same: to establish governance that supports the mission of the church and serves the people God has called it to reach.

A Quick Story

Church governance documents are never really finished. They should be reviewed regularly and embedded into the normal rhythms of church leadership rather than treated as something addressed only during a crisis.

While finishing this book, our church discovered a governance issue in an area where I had done very little prior research. Someone asked a simple question that led our team to review the church's Articles of Incorporation. We soon realized they had been revised only once in the nearly one hundred years since the church's founding.

The version available to us had been typed in the 1970s, and the copy was so difficult to read that one of our team members spent significant time retyping it so we could review it clearly. As we worked through the document, we quickly identified several issues that needed attention. My first call was to our attorney, and we are now revising our Articles of Incorporation.

I share this story for several reasons.

First, Articles of Incorporation are not a major focus of this book, yet they are an important part of church governance and should be reviewed periodically.

Second, governance documents are living documents that require ongoing care. They should be reviewed regularly and updated thoughtfully as churches grow, laws change, and ministry contexts shift.

Third, the issues in our Articles of Incorporation existed long before I came to the church. During that time, God still worked through the ministry in remarkable ways. That reminder matters. Governance problems should be addressed, but they should not cause leaders to lose perspective.

Focusing only on fixing structures, updating policies, and correcting governance documents can distract us from our true mission: the Great Commission. Healthy governance is meant to support that mission, not replace it. Our goal as leaders is not merely to build a well-structured nonprofit, but to lead faithful churches that actively minister to people with the life-changing message of the gospel.

PART I
FOUNDATIONS

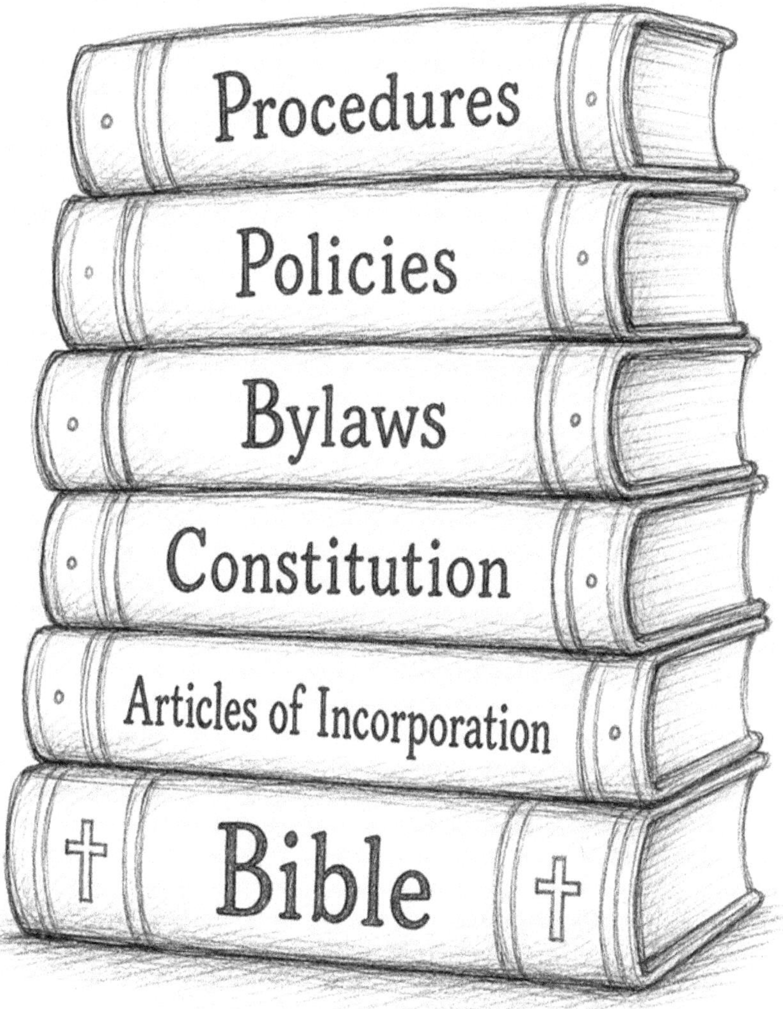

CHAPTER 1

THE IMPORTANCE OF CHURCH GOVERNANCE IN REVITALIZATION

Church revitalization conversations usually focus on vision, preaching, discipleship, and culture. These priorities are essential. Yet many churches that pursue revitalization overlook a quieter factor that often determines whether change will take root or fall apart: governance.

At first glance, governance may seem an unlikely place to begin a conversation about revitalization. Governance rarely excites people. It feels administrative and procedural, disconnected from spiritual vitality. For many church leaders, revitalization feels like a spiritual and cultural challenge, while governance feels like paperwork. Yet throughout Scripture, the ordering of God's people is never separate from their spiritual health. In both the Old and New Testaments, God provides instructions for leadership, accountability, and the care of the flock, showing that how we organize life together reflects our understanding of His authority and our calling to serve with integrity. When we recognize governance as a matter of faithful stewardship, its significance becomes clearly spiritual, not merely administrative.

Yet experience consistently shows that the two are closely connected. Mark Clifton, senior director of replanting at the North American Mission Board, observes, "Many older, dying churches have complex and detailed organizational structures that make the decision-making process slow and unresponsive."[1] When leadership structures become unclear or overly complicated, even healthy ideas struggle to move forward. Vision stalls, decision-making becomes difficult, and leaders often find themselves managing confusion rather than leading change.

As a result, governance issues are often delayed until conflict demands attention. When that occurs, governance shifts from aiding revitalization to becoming a distraction from it.

Looking closely at a church's governing structures often reveals how a church actually functions. The way authority is defined, disagreements are resolved, and decisions are made reflects deeper patterns of trust, leadership, and accountability. In many cases, examining governance becomes one of the clearest ways to understand the true health of a congregation.

Healthy governance is not about control. It is about care. It creates the conditions for leaders to lead well, for congregations to trust the process, and for meaningful change to occur without unnecessary conflict.

For churches seeking revitalization, addressing governance early is not a distraction from revitalization. It is often one of the first steps that allows revitalization to move forward with clarity, trust, and unity.

Framing Governance as Pastoral Care

There are many ways a pastor provides pastoral care for a congregation. Counseling, prayer, hospital visits, encouragement, and faithful presence are all essential expressions of love and shepherding. A church will struggle to thrive without a pastor who makes this kind of care a priority. Most pastors recognize this kind of care instinctively.

Pastoral care, however, also includes concern for the structures that shape a congregation's life together. How authority is exercised, how decisions are made, and how accountability is practiced can either support a church's health or quietly undermine it. When these structures are unclear or unhealthy, they create confusion, anxiety, and conflict that affect the whole body.

In this way, governance itself becomes a pastoral concern. Pastoral care is expressed not only through emotional and spiritual support but also through the responsible stewardship of the organizational systems and decision-making structures that shape the daily life of the church community. By attending to these systems, pastors actively foster an environment where spiritual growth, trust, and communal well-being are more likely to flourish. Thus, effective governance becomes an extension of pastoral responsibility, upholding the congregation's health and unity.

When governance is unclear, people often carry emotional weight tied to church systems rather than spiritual growth. Staff wonder who truly has authority. Committees struggle to know how decisions should be made. Members grow anxious when outcomes feel unpredictable. Over time, this confusion erodes trust, informal power structures emerge, and ministry momentum suffers.

Clear governance is a form of pastoral care because it reduces anxiety. It allows people to serve with confidence rather than fear. It protects leaders from impossible expectations and congregations from unnecessary turmoil.

Good governance does not remove the need for grace. It creates space for it.

In revitalization efforts, churches are often already navigating grief, hope, nostalgia, and uncertainty. Governance clarity helps stabilize those emotions. It encourages the congregation that change is intentional, not impulsive. In this sense, good governance helps sustain revitalization efforts by reducing confusion and strengthening trust.

Why Churches Drift Without "Good" Documents

Churches rarely wake up one day and decide to drift. Drift happens slowly, often unnoticed, when practice replaces principle and memory replaces clarity.

In the absence of clear, current, and consistently followed governing documents, churches rely on informal systems to function. Decisions are guided by phrases such as:

- "This is how we've always done it."
- "So-and-so usually handles that."
- "I think the bylaws say..."

These systems work until they do not, or until someone tries to change something.

As churches grow, decline, or experience leadership transitions, informal practices are strained. New leaders interpret traditions differently. Long-time members remember authority one way, while newer members assume another. Over time, the church's identity and decision-making processes become unclear.

Drift also occurs when churches pursue good goals without defined boundaries. Vision initiatives multiply. Ministries expand. But without governance guardrails, priorities shift quietly. The church may still be busy, but it becomes less aligned.

Good governance documents are clear, current, aligned with actual church practice, and grounded in biblical conviction. Clarity helps leaders and members understand roles, authority, and processes. Alignment ensures that what is written matches how decisions are made day to day. A biblical foundation keeps the church's core documents connected to its faith commitments and mission. While these documents do not automatically prevent drift, they help guard against it. Without them, drift becomes nearly unavoidable.

Can Your Governance Support Revitalization?

Revitalization requires significant change. It may involve renewed prayer, adjusting ministry priorities, reallocating resources, updating staffing structures, revising long-standing practices, reviewing bylaws, or creating new policies. Often, it includes long conversations, difficult decisions, and more prayer than anyone originally expected.

Each of these steps requires authority, trust, and a clear process. When governance systems are outdated, incomplete, or inconsistently followed, even well-intended change becomes difficult to sustain. Momentum slows. Anxiety rises. Leaders hesitate not because they lack vision, but because they lack clarity.

A helpful diagnostic question is simple. If our church needed to make a difficult decision tomorrow, would our governance systems support it?

When the answer is uncertain, governance work becomes part of revitalization rather than a distraction from it.

Churches with healthy governance are better equipped to manage disagreement without division, empower leaders without alienating members, and sustain momentum beyond a single season or a single personality. Governance does not create vision. It protects it.

One reason churches resist formal governance is fear of losing flexibility. Leaders worry that written documents will slow momentum or restrict ministry. In practice, the opposite is often true. A lack of governance usually results in less, not more, flexibility.

When authority is unclear, every decision requires negotiation. When processes are undefined, leaders hesitate. When expectations vary, conflict increases. Over time, fear of backlash replaces confidence, and change becomes harder to pursue.

Healthy governance creates predictable flexibility. It defines who can act, when consultation is needed, and how decisions are reviewed. This clarity allows leaders to move quickly when needed because the boundaries are understood and trusted.

Flexibility without clarity may feel freeing at first, but it often leads to unnecessary mistrust. Clarity, by contrast, creates confidence, and confidence is essential for revitalization to take root. Research professor and author Brené Brown is credited with the simple insight that clarity is kindness. When it comes to the church's foundational systems, this insight rings especially true.

When Governance Is Ignored, Authority Goes Underground

Ignoring governance does not eliminate its influence. It simply pushes it below the surface. Most churches do not intentionally choose this path.

When formal systems are weak or unclear, informal authority naturally fills the gap. Trusted individuals begin to carry influence that is never clearly defined. Decisions are shaped more by relationships than by agreed processes. These patterns usually develop with good intentions and a genuine desire to help the church function.

This dynamic is especially common in churches that have experienced leadership instability. When pastors serve for only a short time, or when a church goes through extended periods without pastoral leadership, informal systems often emerge to provide continuity. In the absence of clear structures, people simply do what seems necessary to keep the church moving forward.

For a time, this arrangement can appear to work. The church continues to function because trusted individuals quietly make decisions behind the scenes. But revitalization exposes the limits of these informal systems.

Revitalization introduces change. New leaders bring fresh direction. Ministries are evaluated. Decisions that were once handled quietly now require broader agreement and clear communication. When authority has been operating informally for years, these moments often create tension. People are unsure who should decide. Long-standing influencers feel displaced. New leaders struggle to lead within systems that were never clearly defined. Instead of supporting revitalization, the absence of clear governance begins to slow it down.

Revitalization requires more than vision and energy. It requires structures that allow leaders to lead, members to trust the process, and decisions to move forward without unnecessary confusion. When governance remains unclear, the weight of leadership increases while trust gradually erodes.

What once served as a temporary workaround can eventually become a barrier to the very revitalization the church is seeking.

Governance as a Ministry of Preparation

Scripture reminds us that preparation matters. In 1 Corinthians 14:40, Paul wrote that "all things should be done decently and in order." Throughout the life of God's people, thoughtful preparation has often preceded seasons of growth and faithfulness. When rightly ordered, structures support good stewardship. Order creates space for growth.

Governance prepares a church for change by clarifying expectations, defining authority, protecting unity, and reducing unnecessary conflict. These are not abstract ideals. They are practical expressions of care that help a congregation move forward together.

This kind of preparation is not unspiritual. It is an act of faithfulness. It reflects trust that God works not only in moments of necessity but also in seasons of careful planning and shared responsibility. Churches that invest in governance before a crisis are not pessimistic. They are wise.

Conclusion

Governance may be under discussed, but it is not insignificant. It quietly shapes how churches operate and navigate change, how leaders exercise authority, and how people learn to trust over time. Whether recognized or not, governance systems are always at work within the life of a church.

Revitalization that overlooks governance is fragile. Governance without a gospel-shaped vision for the church is empty. When a church intentionally brings these together, it creates an environment where leaders can lead with confidence, members can trust the process driven by the systems in place, and the church's mission can endure beyond a single season of pastoral leadership.

As you read this book, the question is not whether your church has a governance structure. The deeper question is whether that structure serves the mission God has entrusted to you to steward.

That work begins here.

Reflection Questions

1. When you think about your church's current governance, what emotions surface most often: confidence, anxiety, uncertainty, or trust? What might those emotions be revealing?
2. If your church needed to make a difficult decision tomorrow, would your current governance provide clarity or create confusion? Why?
3. Where does informal authority currently operate in your church, and how has it helped or hindered trust and ministry?
4. In what ways could clearer governance function as an act of pastoral care in your current context?

CHAPTER 2

BIBLICAL FOUNDATIONS FOR CHURCH GOVERNANCE

This book is not intended to be a comprehensive theology of the church. It does not attempt to resolve any ecclesiological debate or prescribe a single governance model for all congregations. Faithful churches have long differed on matters of polity, structure, and practice. While this chapter lays a biblical and theological foundation, later chapters will offer practical steps for church leaders to apply these principles within their specific contexts.

At the same time, this book is not theologically neutral.

Congregational polity provides the theological framework for the governance approach taken in this book and reflects the convictions expressed in the Baptist Faith and Message. Congregational polity refers to a model of church governance in which final authority for making significant decisions rests with the congregation as a whole, rather than with a hierarchy of leaders or external authorities. This approach emphasizes the responsibility and participation of the entire church body in matters of doctrine, membership, and direction. Within this framework, governance is treated not merely as a practical necessity but as a theological responsibility rooted in stewardship, order, and faithfulness. This chapter establishes why governance matters not only for organizational health but also for the church's witness, mission, and long-term faithfulness.

Humanity, Stewardship, and the Need for Order

Scripture teaches that human beings are created in the image of God and entrusted with stewardship over His creation. This is found throughout various passages of scripture, particularly in Genesis 1:26–28. This is further stated in the Baptist Faith and Message Article III, which summarizes that humanity bears dignity and responsibility, yet Scripture is equally clear that sin affects every aspect of human life, including leadership and decision-making.[2] This tension shapes the life of the church. Leaders are called to faithfulness, yet they remain limited and dependent on grace. Governance is maintained not because people cannot obey, but because effective stewardship depends upon clarity, accountability, and responsibility.

The New Testament confirms that administration is a spiritual gift within the church. Paul states in 1 Corinthians 12:28 that God has granted leadership and administrative gifts to the church body. The Greek word for administration, kubernesis, is akin to the English term helmsman. Just as an experienced helmsman directs a ship through challenging waters, church leaders in administrative roles are essential in guiding the congregation toward its unique mission. Governance is therefore not a permitted deviation from righteousness; rather, it serves as a way for pastors to faithfully steward the church in a fallen world. Like a ship's navigator avoiding hidden dangers, pastors steer their congregations with the tools given to them, helping the church navigate faithfully amid the hazards of a fallen world.

The Nature of the Church

Any discussion of governance must be grounded in a biblical understanding of the church.

The New Testament depicts the church as the Body of Christ, made up of redeemed individuals who come together for worship, discipleship, fellowship, and mission. Harwood explains that even "though some New Testament texts refer to the church in a universal sense, most of the verses refer to local churches."[3] Local churches are not abstract institutions. They are embodied communities of real people entrusted with real responsibility and called to make real decisions. Ecclesiology must therefore address how churches actually function, not only what they affirm.

Christ's relationship to the church establishes both authority and care. Jesus speaks of the church as His own, declaring in Matthew 16:18, when speaking to Peter, "I will build my church..." In Ephesians 5:25, Paul describes Christ's love for the church as self-giving and sacrificial, much like the way a husband should love their wife. These passages confirm that the church is Christ's, not owned by its leaders, members, or traditions. Because the church belongs to Christ, authority must be exercised carefully and stewarded faithfully. Governance flows from this reality. Governance exists to reflect Christ's care for His church, not to replace it.

The Mission of the Church and the Need for Order

The church's mission is clearly defined in the Great Commission found in Matthew 28:18–20. The church exists to make disciples, baptize believers, and teach obedience to Christ. Governance does not replace this mission. It supports and protects it.

In the New Testament book of Acts, the early church provides a clear example of structure serving mission. Acts 2:46–47 describes believers gathering regularly, sharing life together, and organizing their ministry in ways that supported unity and growth. Then later in Acts 6:1–7, when conflict arose over the care of widows, the apostles clarified roles and established a process that allowed ministry to continue without distraction. This was not a retreat from spiritual priorities. It was a faithful response that protected them.

Paul, in 1 Corinthians 14:40, reinforces this principle when he instructs the Corinthian church that "all things should be done decently and in order." He grounds this instruction in God's character in 1 Corinthians 14:33, reminding them that God is not a God of confusion but of peace.

Order within the church does not conflict with the work of the Spirit. When rightly practiced, it can support unity, reduce confusion, and help the church remain focused on its mission.

Southern Baptist Convictions and Local Church Responsibility

Southern Baptist ecclesiology found in the Baptist Faith and Message Article VI, emphasizes the autonomy of the local church, regenerate church membership, and congregational responsibility under the lordship of Christ.[4]

Within this Southern Baptist framework, grounded in Baptist principles such as congregational polity, local church autonomy, and the priesthood of all believers, this book approaches church governance from a congregational perspective. These theological convictions shape governance by establishing the congregation as the ultimate authority under the lordship of Christ, even as leadership roles and decision-making structures may vary. Local church autonomy, rooted in Baptist principles, does not indicate a lack of structure; rather, it emphasizes that faithful governance is the congregation's collective responsibility. This theological stance requires churches to clarify how authority is delegated, how decisions are made, and how accountability is maintained, ensuring that all governance practices align with both Scripture and Baptist distinctives.

When a church is in good order, its focus does not waver from accomplishing the Great Commission. Paul's letter to the church in Ephesus, as written in Ephesians 3:10, served as an encouragement, emphasizing that "through the church, the manifold wisdom of God might now be made known to the rulers and authorities in the heavenly places." Herschel Hobbs said, "There are many worthy causes and institutions through which one may labor in the community. Nevertheless, this should not be done at the expense of one's responsibility in and through one's church. The good must not become the enemy of the best."[5] The church, comprised of regenerate believers sent out with the support of other believers, is God's plan to bring the good news of the gospel to the nations.

The Character of God, Order, and Governance

The attributes of God further ground the church's pursuit of order and clarity. "The attributes that classical Christian theology sets forth include holiness, eternality, omniscience (all-knowing), omnipotence (all-powerful), omnipresence (present to all), and goodness. Scripture reveals God as holy, eternal, omniscient, omnipotent, and good."[6] These attributes shape how God relates to His creation. God's providence demonstrates His ordered engagement in the world, guiding history in line with His plans. Throughout Scripture, God provides structure for His people. From the instructions given to Noah to the organization of Israel under Moses to the guidance offered to early churches by the apostles, God consistently works through order rather than chaos. This pattern does not suggest that God is constrained by order. Rather, it reveals that order is one means by which God accomplishes His purposes.

When churches reflect this order through faithful governance, they bear witness to a God who is neither arbitrary nor unclear but purposeful and trustworthy. Good governance, therefore, is not only a practical concern for organizational effectiveness. It is a theological responsibility.

- Because humanity is entrusted with stewardship, governance matters.
- Because the church belongs to Christ, governance matters.
- Because the mission of the church endures across generations, governance matters.
- Because God Himself is a God of order, governance matters.

This book does not advocate a single governance model. Faithful churches throughout history have used a variety of governance structures, including elder-led, Presbyterian, Episcopal, and various forms of congregational polity. Each of these models has been used by churches seeking to follow biblical principles in their unique contexts. While this book seeks to help churches develop governance documents and practices that reflect biblical faithfulness and practical clarity, leaders from other traditions are encouraged to thoughtfully adapt the principles discussed here in ways that honor their own denominational convictions and settings.

Conclusion

Church governance goes beyond simply technical procedures. It reflects a church's beliefs concerning God, authority, stewardship, and responsibility. Whether acknowledged or not, theology shapes decision-making and leadership approaches. For churches aiming for health or revitalization, this theological foundation is crucial. Structures that are not aligned with biblical convictions may struggle to adapt to change. Governance rooted in a clear grasp of the church's nature and mission offers stability amid changing circumstances.

The chapters that follow move from doctrine to practice. Constitutions, bylaws, policies, and procedures are not replacements for theological faithfulness. They are expressions of it. When grounded in Scripture and driven by conviction, effective governance documents should support the church's mission rather than detract from it.

Reflection Questions

1. How do your church's current governance practices reflect what you believe about the nature of the church and Christ's authority over it?
2. In what ways might unexamined theology be shaping how decisions are made in your church, for better or for worse?
3. How comfortable is your church with order and structure as expressions of faithfulness rather than obstacles to spiritual vitality?
4. As your church navigates change or revitalization, where might a clearer theological grounding strengthen confidence and unity?

CHAPTER 3

CONSTITUTION: THE FOUNDATION

A church constitution may seem like a heavy, formal document. Some leaders treat it as timeless. Others avoid it entirely. Still others confuse it with bylaws, policies, or long-standing traditions whose origins have been forgotten.

The good news is that a constitution does not have to be complicated or inaccessible. When written clearly, it can serve as a helpful and understandable resource that protects the church's identity and supports the congregation's life together.

Before a church decides whether it needs a constitution, it should ask a more basic question: What is a constitution actually meant to do?

What a Church Constitution Is (and Isn't)

At its core, a constitution serves as one of the church's foundational governing documents. It captures the commitments a congregation believes should remain steady over time, even as leadership changes, ministries evolve, or cultural pressures shift. Before addressing how decisions are made, a constitution helps answer a more basic question: who are we as a church?

Historically, church constitutions often took shape during seasons when denominations were forming, doctrines were being clarified, or churches were trying to guard against theological drift. As churches became more formally organized and recognized as legal nonprofit entities, written constitutions helped clarify governance, define responsibility, and provide organizational stability. These documents typically included statements of faith, purpose, and authority that were intentionally difficult to amend. The aim was not rigidity, but stability, protecting a church's identity while allowing ministry methods to change over time.

Today, however, the word constitution is used in a variety of ways. Some churches use it to refer to a single document that covers everything from doctrinal commitments to meeting procedures. Others use the term more informally, referring to shared assumptions about how things have always been done. Still others have a constitution, but it lives quietly in a filing cabinet, rarely referenced and likely out of step with current practice.

It is also important to recognize that a church does not need a document titled "constitution" in order to function faithfully. Many healthy churches operate under a well-constructed set of bylaws that accomplish the same purpose. The real issue is not what the document is called, but whether the church's foundational commitments are clearly stated and appropriately protected.

A healthy constitution avoids regulating daily ministry activity or procedural details. When operational matters are placed into a constitution, the document becomes difficult to amend and eventually ignored. The most effective constitutions tend to be concise, durable, and authoritative, focusing on the core commitments that define the church and provide continuity across generations of leadership.

The Difference Between a Constitution and Articles of Incorporation

One of the more common points of confusion in church governance is understanding the difference between a constitution and articles of incorporation. Both documents are important, but they serve very different purposes.

Articles of Incorporation are civil documents created when a church forms a legal entity under state law. They establish the church's legal existence and provide certain rights and protections recognized by the state. These articles typically include the church's legal name, stated purpose, duration, registered agent, and provisions for handling assets if the organization were dissolved. Once filed, the Articles of Incorporation carry legal authority that cannot be overridden by internal church documents. Because state laws vary, churches should review their Articles of Incorporation with qualified legal counsel before making changes.

A constitution serves a different role. It does not create the church's legal existence. Instead, it functions as an internal governing document that helps define how the church understands itself and how authority is exercised within the congregation. In simple terms, articles of incorporation answer to the state, while a constitution answers to the church.

Confusion arises when these distinctions become blurred. It is easy to assume that constitutions carry greater legal authority than articles of incorporation. It is also easy to unintentionally place doctrinal or governance language directly into their articles, not realizing that doing so can make future changes unnecessarily difficult under state law.

Healthy governance recognizes that these documents work together within a clear hierarchy:

- Articles of Incorporation
- Constitution
- Bylaws
- Policies
- Procedures

Understanding this hierarchy helps protect a church from unintended limitations and prevents conflicts between documents that were never intended to compete. When each document serves its proper role, governance becomes clearer and far easier to maintain over time.

Essential Components of a Church Constitution

Church constitutions are not identical, and they should not be. Churches differ in their histories, sizes, cultures, denominations, and ministry contexts, which often shape the tone and content of their governing documents. Nonetheless, most effective constitutions cover a common set of core areas. These elements are intentionally concise and emphasize what defines the church rather than the specifics of daily ministry operations.

Legal Name and Purpose

Most constitutions begin with the church's name and purpose. This section identifies the congregation and, in simple terms, explains why the church exists. The language typically reflects the church's commitment to worship, proclaiming the gospel, making disciples, and carrying out its mission. Because a constitution is meant to endure, many churches ground this purpose in the Great Commission, often citing Matthew 28:18–20 rather than relying on a ministry mission statement that may evolve over time.

Statement of Faith

A constitution often includes a statement of faith. Many Baptist churches adopt a formal confession, such as the Baptist Faith and Message. The goal is not to provide an exhaustive theological explanation but to clearly express the beliefs that shape teaching, leadership, and cooperation. Because doctrinal unity matters deeply to a congregation's life, churches often place these commitments in a document that requires thoughtful, often difficult consideration before any changes are made.

Church Covenant

Many constitutions define membership at a basic level, outlining who belongs to the church and how members commit to living together in Christian community. This is often called a membership covenant. It typically sets membership requirements, such as baptism, and outlines expectations for participation, responsibility, and spiritual accountability. Some churches also include a church covenant that explains how members agree to walk together in Christian love, pursue spiritual growth, and care for one another. Although covenant language may seem traditional, its purpose is practical—reminding the congregation that membership is about shared life and mutual commitment. Detailed membership procedures are usually found in bylaws, while the constitution describes the church's understanding of belonging.

Leadership Roles

Another important component involves governance and authority. This section helps clarify how leadership functions within the church and how authority is exercised. Roles such as pastors, deacons, elders, and trustees may be identified, along with the congregation's responsibility for affirming leadership and major decisions. In congregational churches, especially, this clarity helps prevent confusion about who is responsible for what and how decisions are ultimately made.

Dissolution Clause

Nearly every constitution includes a dissolution clause, stating that if the church were ever to cease operations, its assets would be transferred to another nonprofit or ministry organization rather than distributed to individuals. While rarely discussed, this provision protects both the church's mission and its charitable purpose.[7]

Amendment Process

Since constitutions are meant to ensure lasting stability, they thoughtfully include an amendment process that is vigilant and often tedious. Advance notice, supermajority approval, or multiple readings are common safeguards. These measures are not meant to prevent change, but to ensure that foundational commitments are revised thoughtfully rather than in response to momentary pressure.

Denominational Affiliation

For churches cooperating with the Southern Baptist Convention or similar networks, constitutions often include language affirming shared doctrinal commitments and cooperative ministry relationships. Such statements help clarify partnership while preserving local church autonomy.

A healthy constitution focuses on what must endure. It should be clear enough for members to understand, stable enough for leaders to trust, and limited enough not to attempt to manage everyday ministry decisions. When a constitution serves this purpose well, it provides continuity across generations. As stated above, a church constitution should be as short as possible and easy to understand.

Approaching Constitutional Change Wisely

For churches considering adopting or revising a constitution, the process often matters as much as the document itself. Constitutional changes naturally raise questions of identity, authority, and trust. When handled poorly, they can create unnecessary tension. When approached thoughtfully, however, they can strengthen unity and bring much-needed clarity.

Education should come before action. Congregations benefit from understanding what a constitution is and why it matters long before they are asked to vote on any changes. Teaching moments, written explanations, and open conversations help members participate with confidence rather than uncertainty. Leaders can provide practical education through regular Q&A sessions during scheduled meetings, brief teaching series on church governance, or handouts that explain key differences between constitutions and bylaws. It is equally important to clearly distinguish between the role of constitutional matters and that of other governance documents. Without that distinction, churches often include too much detail in the constitution simply because a concern feels urgent at the time. Over time, this leads to documents that are difficult to amend and gradually ignored.

Pacing the process wisely is just as important. Constitutional change rarely benefits from urgency. Allowing space for questions, feedback, and reflection helps build trust and reduce anxiety within the congregation.

Ultimately, churches should anticipate that constitutional discussions might surface long-buried issues. These conversations often reveal differing expectations, authority structures, or theological perspectives. Although such moments may feel uncomfortable, they provide essential opportunities for congregations to critically examine their assumptions, clarify misunderstandings, and address sources of tension directly. By engaging openly with discomfort, church leaders and members can enact practical steps to strengthen mutual understanding and build a more resilient, unified community.

Do Churches Need a Constitution?

Churches are generally not required to maintain a constitution. Courts do not mandate one, and in many states, constitutions and bylaws are treated similarly. Courts instead tend to examine whether a church consistently follows its own governing documents and established procedures.

When legal disputes arise, courts typically look to a church's highest governing authority to determine how decisions are meant to be made. For churches without a constitution, that role is usually fulfilled by the bylaws. For churches that maintain both a constitution and bylaws, problems can arise when the relationship between the two documents is unclear or when their provisions overlap or contradict. For this reason, churches that choose to maintain both documents should ensure that:

- The relationship between the constitution and bylaws is clearly defined.
- Amendment processes reflect the different levels of authority assigned to each document.
- Language is carefully coordinated so the documents support rather than compete with one another.

The legal concern is rarely the absence of a constitution. More often, risk arises when governing documents are unclear, inconsistent, or selectively followed.

For example, courts have sometimes ruled against churches that failed to follow their stated procedures during leadership disputes, even when churches had governing documents in place. Clarity and consistency provide far greater protection than terminology alone.

Case Study: When Foundations Are Assumed

A church had operated for decades without a clearly defined constitution. Leaders regularly cited "what the constitution says," even though no current copy could be found. Over the years, the bylaws had been revised several times, often to address immediate needs, without anyone realizing that those revisions were beginning to conflict with assumptions about governing authority.

The tension remained largely unnoticed until a leadership change prompted the church to face difficult decisions. Soon, questions arose about who had the authority to act and the process for making decisions. Various groups referenced their understanding of the church constitution, only to discover that no one could verify what the document actually specified.

What began as disagreement soon became confusion, and that confusion eventually led to conflict. The church ultimately found itself forced to reconstruct its governing framework under significant pressure, rather than through thoughtful planning.

Much of the conflict could have been avoided if the church had clarified its documents earlier. Instead, assumptions quietly replaced clarity, and tradition took the place of documentation.

Situations like this serve as a reminder to church leaders that when governance is taken for granted and not clearly defined, it can become a source of conflict during times of change.

Conclusion

Having a constitution does not necessarily mean a church is thriving, nor does its absence imply neglect. What really matters is whether the church has clearly defined and effectively protected its core commitments that shape its life and governance. The importance lies more in the clarity, consistency, and faithful application of these commitments than in whether they are written in a constitution or bylaws. Churches that dedicate time to establishing and regularly reviewing these principles are working to promote faithfulness, unity, and long-term sustainability in ministry. Well-defined governing documents provide confidence to future leaders and congregations, enabling them to proceed with the assurance that their most important values have been thoughtfully outlined.

Constitution Review Checklist

A healthy church constitution is designed to provide clarity and stability rather than unnecessary complexity. The following questions are intended to help leaders thoughtfully evaluate the effectiveness of their current constitution. These questions serve not as a test to pass, but as a guide for reflection and conversation.

Identity and Purpose

- Does our constitution clearly state the church's official name and purpose?

- Does it describe why our church exists rather than how ministry is currently organized?

Doctrinal Clarity

- Does the constitution include a clear statement of faith or doctrinal affirmation?
- Are these doctrinal commitments protected through a careful amendment process?
- Does the constitution address the church's relationship with a denomination or a fellowship of churches?

Membership Foundations

- Does it define who may become a member of the church?
- Does it establish basic membership expectations without including procedures better suited to bylaws?

Governance and Authority

- Does the constitution clarify where authority ultimately rests within the church?
- Are leadership roles identified at a foundational level without regulating daily ministry operations?

Amendment Process

- Are constitutional changes intentionally thoughtful rather than easily made?
- Does the amendment process allow necessary change while protecting foundational commitments?

Appropriate Scope

- Is the constitution focused on enduring principles rather than ministry procedures?
- Could an average church member reasonably understand the document?

CHAPTER 4

BYLAWS: THE MAIN THINGS

Since a constitution defines the church's foundational identity, bylaws explain how the church's authority and decision-making are structured. They do not exist to inspire vision or manage every ministry detail. They provide the governing framework that guides meetings, leadership selection, accountability, and major decisions. They provide the governing framework for meetings, leadership selection, accountability, staff-related authority, and major decisions, especially during moments of tension or conflict. They explicitly specify how authority should be exercised in daily circumstances, assuring everyone understands the appropriate course of action.

Many churches view bylaws as technical or tedious, something to reference only when necessary. In reality, they are among the most pastoral documents a church possesses. Clear, well-structured bylaws reduce confusion, steady expectations, and protect unity long before conflict ever appears. When they are unclear or inconsistently followed, trust begins to erode quietly, often without anyone noticing until tension has already grown.

This chapter explains what bylaws are designed to do, what they are not meant to control, and how churches can avoid common mistakes that make bylaws ineffective. Good bylaws do not complicate ministry. They make a healthy ministry more sustainable.

Defining Bylaws: What They Are and What They Aren't

Bylaws serve as the main set of governing rules for a church's internal operations. They explain how decisions are made, who has the authority to make them, and how leaders are selected, evaluated, and, when necessary, removed. Unlike a constitution, which is meant to remain relatively stable, bylaws are expected to evolve over time as a church grows, adapts, and refines its systems.

Bylaws are often misunderstood. They are not policies, nor are they procedural for every ministry detail or operational decision. Policies address what should happen in specific areas of church life, and procedures outline how those policies are carried out. When those operational details are embedded in bylaws, the document becomes overly complex, difficult to amend, and eventually neglected.

They are not vision documents either. Bylaws do not exist to inspire or cast direction for the future. Instead, they provide structure so that vision can be pursued without confusion or unnecessary power struggles. Healthy governance quietly supports mission; it does not compete with it.

Bylaws also do not replace trust. No document can do that. But they do provide guardrails when trust is strained. In healthy churches, bylaws are rarely consulted because clarity prevents crisis. In struggling churches, they are often rediscovered during moments of tension, sometimes revealing gaps or ambiguities that were never addressed.

Well-written bylaws tend to answer a consistent set of practical questions:

- Who ultimately holds authority in the church?
- How are leaders selected and, if necessary, removed?
- How are decisions made and properly documented?
- What processes govern meetings, voting, and accountability?

Effective bylaws are clear enough to follow, flexible enough to adapt, and restrained enough to remain readable. When they fulfill this role effectively, they operate quietly in support of the church's functions.

Why Bylaws Matter in Moments of Conflict

Most churches rarely review their bylaws until an issue arises. For example, a congregation might not revisit the bylaws for years, only to consult them urgently during a dispute over pastoral succession or a contentious decision by the governing board. In times of peace, the bylaws quietly sit in the background. However, when disagreements arise or leadership transitions become complicated, bylaws suddenly take on considerable importance.

In many legal disputes, courts may look to a church's bylaws as evidence of the agreement between the church and its members.[8] Judges are not concerned with what leaders hoped to do or what the church usually does. They look to the bylaws and whether the church has followed them consistently.

For this reason, inconsistency can be more damaging than weakness. A church with imperfect bylaws but consistent practice may fare better than a church with strong language that is routinely ignored.

There are a few important principles worth understanding.

Courts usually defer to churches on doctrinal issues, but not on procedural matters. When disputes involve governance, membership status, or leadership authority, courts often apply the "neutral principles of law." This means they evaluate whether the church followed its own established rules without attempting to interpret theology.[9]

Bylaws should also comply with applicable nonprofit law. In many states, if bylaws are silent on an issue, default provisions in state law may apply. Churches are sometimes surprised to discover that when their documents do not address a matter clearly, the law may fill the gap in ways they never anticipated. For this reason, it is wise for churches to consult legal counsel when drafting or revising their bylaws. An attorney familiar with nonprofit and church law can help ensure that a church's documents meet legal requirements and avoid misunderstandings or unintended consequences in the future.

Clarity matters as well. Vague language such as "as determined appropriate" or "at the discretion of leadership" may feel flexible and pastoral, but it can create confusion when examined closely. Clear processes demonstrate fairness and consistency, protecting both leaders and the congregation.

Finally, bylaws should be treated as living documents. This does not mean they change frequently, but that they should be reviewed intentionally and updated as needed. A good practice is to set a regular review interval, such as every two or three years, so the document is revisited before issues arise. Involving a diverse group of church leaders and members in this process can reveal practical needs and promote ownership of any changes. Outdated bylaws are among the most common governance vulnerabilities churches face.

Clear bylaws are not indications of distrust; rather, they serve as tools to preserve unity during periods when trust is challenged.

Common Bylaw Issues

Most bylaw problems are not the result of bad intentions. They usually emerge during seasons of growth, transition, or simple neglect. Over time, patterns develop that many churches eventually recognize in hindsight.

One common failure occurs when bylaws reflect a church that no longer exists. A congregation grows, adds staff, adjusts its leadership structure, or changes how meetings are conducted, yet the bylaws remain frozen in an earlier season. Eventually, leaders begin operating outside the document simply to keep the ministry moving. What begins as practicality slowly becomes precedent, and the church is unintentionally trained to disregard its own governing rules.

Another frequent issue involves unclear lines of authority. When bylaws do not clearly define who is responsible for staff, finances, or ministry direction, power struggles often follow. Authority rarely remains vacant. If it is not clearly defined, it will be assumed, and those differing assumptions can quietly strain relationships. What begins as uncertainty about responsibility can gradually erode trust among leaders and create confusion within the congregation.

A third failure is overloading bylaws with operational detail. Including job descriptions, ministry procedures, or policy-level decisions makes the document difficult to amend and easy to violate. Bylaws should clarify who makes decisions, not dictate how every decision is carried out.

Some churches face challenges with duplicated or conflicting documents. Repeated provisions across constitutions, bylaws, and policies can gradually become misaligned. When disagreements arise, leaders often struggle to identify the governing document, which can worsen tensions rather than resolve them.

Finally, many churches never establish or communicate a clear amendment process. When members do not understand how bylaws can be revised, proposed changes can feel threatening. Clarity builds trust. Uncertainty often breeds suspicion.

A clear amendment process typically outlines the basic steps for amending the bylaws. This may include submitting a written amendment proposal, ensuring the proposal is communicated to the congregation or decision-making body in advance, providing an opportunity for discussion or questions, and then holding a formal vote that meets a specified requirement (such as a two-thirds majority). By defining and sharing these steps, the church helps everyone understand how revisions are made and reassures members that changes will happen transparently and fairly.

These failures do not indicate weak leadership. Instead, they serve as reminders that governance, much like ministry, demands consistent attention and continuous, deliberate upkeep.

Case Study: When Good Intentions Create Bad Bylaws

A growing church revised its bylaws during a period of rapid expansion. As new ministries launched and staff were added, the revision committee sought to empower leaders to act swiftly. To promote flexibility, the committee included language granting "broad authority" to staff and ministry boards without explicitly defining the scope of that authority. At the time, confidence was high, and the revisions were adopted unanimously.

Several years later, a leadership transition revealed the limitations of that language. New leaders interpreted "broad authority" differently from the original authors. Members who felt excluded from certain decisions appealed to the bylaws, only to find that the document offered little clarity.

The conflict that followed was not rooted in doctrine or personality. It was structural. Both parties believed they were acting faithfully. However, in the absence of explicit boundaries within the bylaws, there was no common framework for resolving disagreements. Ultimately, the church amended its bylaws amidst the conflict, a process that proved significantly more challenging than a careful revision conducted years earlier.

The fundamental lesson was not one of mistrust but of foresight. Clarity in one season protects the church in the next.

Conclusion

Bylaws might not be exciting, but they are essential. They connect a church's core values with daily choices. Good bylaws do not prevent conflict; they help manage it by setting shared expectations and clear procedures before issues arise. Churches that manage their bylaws effectively are not opting for rigidity over relationships. Instead, they favor clarity over confusion and trust over assumptions. This clarity allows leaders to avoid constant re-negotiation of authority, enabling steady and confident progress in ministry.

Undertaking the work of reviewing, maintaining, and applying bylaws is a vital act of stewardship for church leaders. Your careful oversight in this area honors both your congregation and your calling by safeguarding the church's unity, mission, and witness for the future. Though this work can be complex and, at times, challenging, it is a meaningful expression of leadership that serves the whole body.

Evaluating the Health of Your Church's Bylaws

As you reflect on your church's bylaws, consider the following:

- Do our bylaws reflect how our church actually functions today, or do they describe a previous season?
- Are lines of authority clearly defined, especially during leadership transitions?
- Do our bylaws clearly distinguish between the governance structure and operational details?
- Would our leaders and members know where to look in the event of disagreement?
- When was the last time our bylaws were reviewed intentionally rather than reactively?
- If conflict arose tomorrow, would our bylaws provide clarity or confusion?

CHAPTER 5

POLICIES: WHAT SHOULD HAPPEN

"Policies are not merely formal abstract legal clauses, but statements of how we can best work, worship, and minister together in this family." Lynn Buzzard[10]

Within church governance, constitutions define the organizational identity, while bylaws specify lines of authority. Building on these, policies offer practical guidance by answering the common weekly question: What should happen in this situation?

Most churches already operate under policies, whether written or not. Someone knows who can approve expenses. Someone decides who is allowed to serve in children's ministry. Someone determines how conflicts are addressed, how facilities are used, or what to do when an emergency interrupts a normal Sunday. The real question is not whether policies exist. It is whether they are clear, consistently applied, and formally affirmed, or simply assumed and unevenly practiced. For instance, in some congregations, one group of volunteers may be required to complete background checks while another is permitted to begin serving immediately, leading to confusion and perceived unfairness. Such inconsistencies highlight the challenges that arise when policies are informal or not universally enforced.

Policies are not about control. They are about consistency. They help ensure that similar situations are handled in similar ways, not based on personality, pressure, or preference, but with fairness and clarity.

This chapter explains what policies are meant to do, how they differ from procedures, and why written policies matter in the daily life of the church. Good policies do not create bureaucracy. They help churches make decisions consistently, fairly, and with care.

Clarifying Policies Versus Procedures

One of the most common governance mistakes churches make is confusing policies with procedures. The two are closely connected, but they operate at different levels and serve different purposes. When that distinction becomes blurred, unnecessary tension often follows.

A policy defines expectations and boundaries. It answers the question, What should happen, and who has the authority to ensure it happens? Policies establish principles, permissions, limitations, and accountability. They are written broadly enough to guide decisions even in situations that were not specifically anticipated.

By contrast, a procedure explains how a policy is implemented in a specific setting. Procedures provide step-by-step guidance, checklists, or workflows that help staff and volunteers implement policies consistently from week to week. Policies are stable, while procedures are relatively easy to adapt to changing ministry needs.

For example, a policy may require that all individuals serving with minors complete a background check and training. The procedure explains how background checks are requested, who processes them, how often they are renewed, and where records are stored. If the church changes vendors or updates its tracking system, the procedure may shift. The policy does not.

When churches mix policies and procedures, issues arise. Policies tend to become cluttered with operational details and inflexible. Procedures may seem untouchable, causing leaders to avoid minor changes because "it's in the policy," even if the original intent was less specific. Healthy churches set policies based on authority levels and procedures based on execution levels. Maintaining this distinction preserves flexibility while ensuring accountability. This balance allows leaders to adapt to changing needs without weakening shared standards.

Critical Policy Categories

Instead of attempting to document every possible scenario that might someday require a policy, churches should focus on the areas or categories that most directly impact property, personnel, safety, finance, and decision-making authority.

Policies should not be treated as one-size-fits-all. While policy categories may apply broadly across churches, the specific language, structure, and level of detail should reflect the church's size, culture, leadership structure, and polity. A rural congregation with a small staff may not require the same documentation as a multi-site church with multiple ministry layers. The goal is not to duplicate what another church has written, but to practice thoughtful stewardship within your own context. Good governance is always applied locally, even when the principles behind it are widely shared.

While policies should be customized to each congregation's specific needs, these broad categories can help guide effective policy development that all congregations should consider. The main focus should be on clarity, especially in areas relating to property, personnel, safety, finance, and decision-making authority. Clear policies are crucial because any ambiguity in these areas can lead to unnecessary risks. Policies are not meant to create bureaucracy but to safeguard individuals, steward resources wisely, and ensure consistency throughout different ministry phases.

Governance and Authority Policies

These policies clarify how decisions are made within the framework formed by the bylaws. They may define delegated authority, committee responsibilities, staff leadership roles, or approval thresholds for major actions.

Without these policies, churches often rely more on personalities than process. Decisions can feel inconsistent. Leaders may unintentionally exceed their authority or hesitate when clarity is needed. Clear governance policies protect both initiative and accountability.

Financial Stewardship Policies

Financial policies are among the most critical and most commonly underdeveloped. These typically address budgeting processes, spending authority, internal controls, handling contributions, restricted gifts, reimbursements, and audits.

Strong financial policies protect not only the church but also the integrity of those entrusted with stewardship. They reduce suspicion, remove unnecessary temptation, and provide transparency in how resources are managed.

Personnel and Volunteer Policies

Churches often devote considerable care to hiring staff, yet provide minimal written guidance once employment begins. Personnel policies clarify expectations related to hiring, evaluation, discipline, termination, compensation, benefits, and conduct. In many churches, these policies are best organized in a personnel policy manual or employee handbook, especially as staff teams grow. Even smaller congregations benefit from written clarity. Clear expectations protect both the church and the staff member, reducing confusion and providing a shared understanding of responsibilities and accountability.

Safety and Risk Management Policies

Few policy gaps carry higher risks than those related to safety. Policies covering child and student protection, background checks, emergency response, medical incidents, and crisis communication are essential. Having these policies does not imply distrust; instead, they reflect care. Churches that implement safety policies demonstrate love for their congregation and a strong sense of stewardship.

Facility and Property Use Policies

Church buildings are shared spaces. Policies clarify who may use facilities, under what conditions, with whose approval, and with what expectations for responsibility. As churches open their doors to community use, the absence of written guidelines often leads to misunderstanding, damage, or conflict.

Communication and Records Policies

In a digital world, churches handle sensitive information daily. Policies governing communication standards, social media use, technology and artificial intelligence use, data privacy, and records retention help protect individuals and the church's witness. Clarity on access, responsibility, and confidentiality prevents avoidable problems and reinforces trust.

Writing Policies That Serve the Church

Policies serve the church best when they are written clearly and purposefully. Good policies use accessible, understandable language. They avoid unnecessary legal jargon while remaining precise where it matters. They clearly state who holds authority and how decisions are made. For example, a well-crafted facility use policy would outline not only the approval process for outside groups but also who is responsible for oversight and the expectations for use. Such policies are adopted through the appropriate governance process and, just as importantly, actively communicated to those affected through practical methods, making sure they are understood and used rather than merely stored without reference.

Policies should be reviewed intentionally and on a regular schedule through a structured process, overseen by a designated group such as the board, a policy committee, or senior staff, depending on the church's governance structure. Establishing an annual or biennial review led by this group ensures that policies are evaluated against current ministry practices, legal requirements, and organizational changes. During this review, seeking input from legal counsel or denominational resources helps maintain compliance with applicable laws. Assigning clear responsibility simplifies the review process and enables leaders to address necessary updates or clarifications, preserving policy relevance and supporting trust in church governance.

Most importantly, policies should be written with people in mind. They exist to guide behavior, not to punish mistakes. Clear policies reduce anxiety by clarifying expectations. When policies are framed as tools for care rather than instruments of control, they are far more likely to be understood, respected, and followed.

Case Study: When "Everyone Knew" Wasn't Enough

For years, a church operated with an informal understanding that outside groups could use the church building with staff approval. There was no written policy. It had simply always been handled that way, and it seemed to work.

One weekend, however, a community group used the facility for an event that resulted in property damage and an injury. As questions surfaced about who had approved the event and what expectations had been communicated, leaders realized there was no documented process, no signed agreement, and no clearly defined authority. Each person involved remembered the arrangement differently. When the insurance carrier became involved, it was unclear whether the use had been formally authorized at all.

The issue did not stem from a lack of hospitality, as the church demonstrated a sincere commitment to serving its community. Rather, the challenge was rooted in a lack of clarity. For instance, without a written facility use policy specifying who was authorized to approve events, what expectations applied to external groups regarding property use, and what liability conditions were required, responsibilities became ambiguous. If such a policy had existed, it would have stipulated that any outside group must sign an agreement outlining the terms of use and designate a contact person responsible for adherence, thereby ensuring all parties were aware of their obligations and reducing the likelihood of confusion or disputes following an incident.

What was once perceived as flexibility suddenly seemed like vulnerability.

Conclusion

Policies turn authority into action. They give practical expression to the church's core commitments in everyday decisions. Without written policies, churches often rely on memory, personality, and past practice. While those may work for a time, they seldom hold steady through leadership transitions or seasons of growth.

Good policies do not remove the need for wisdom, nor should they attempt to. Instead, they provide a shared framework for making decisions consistently and thoughtfully. That clarity reduces uncertainty and frees leaders to focus on ministry rather than repeatedly renegotiating expectations.

In the next chapter, we turn to procedures. These practical steps bring policies to life and enable churches to act with clarity and confidence in real time.

Reflecting on Your Church's Policies

As you consider your church's current policies, reflect on the following questions:

- Are our most important policies written, approved, and accessible, or do they exist primarily in memory?
- Do our policies reflect how our church actually operates today?

- Have we clearly distinguished between policies and procedures?
- Are authority lines clear within our governance and financial policies?
- Do our personnel and volunteer policies protect both the church and those who serve?
- Have our safety policies been reviewed recently, especially those related to children and vulnerable adults?
- If a leadership transition occurred tomorrow, would our policies provide clarity or confusion?

These questions are not intended to cause concern; rather, they are designed to encourage proactive reflection and foster a sense of responsibility among church leaders and members. By considering them, churches can identify specific areas where existing policies may need clarification, updating, or formalization.

To move from reflection to action, consider these first steps:

- Schedule a policy review meeting in the next quarter to begin evaluating your current policies.
- Appoint a policy coordinator or small team to oversee the review and update process.
- Ensure all approved policies are organized in a central, accessible location and are effectively communicated to relevant leaders and volunteers.

Taking these steps can strengthen trust and support a healthy governance culture within the congregation.

CHAPTER 6

PROCEDURES: FROM POLICY TO PRACTICE

Policies outline what should happen in a church, while procedures explain how those expectations are carried out when the church gathers and ministries are active.

This distinction is important because most governance failures do not stem from poor policy. Instead, they arise when well-crafted policies are left unaddressed and disconnected from daily ministry routines. In many churches, the tension quietly builds between written policies and actual practice. Procedures help close this gap by turning expectations into routines and principles into consistent actions.

Healthy procedures are meant to support ministry staff and volunteers, not restrict them. They help reduce uncertainty and boost confidence. Well-crafted procedures quietly aid daily operations, but unclear or missing ones can lead to frustration, hesitation, or inaction.

Implementing Policies into Everyday Practice

Every policy needs a clear pathway for implementation. Without one, staff and volunteers are left to interpret expectations on their own, often resulting in uneven application. Procedures provide that pathway.

To move from policy to practice, leaders should involve those who will actually use the procedure. A small team can review the relevant policy, outline the necessary steps, test the process in a limited setting, and adjust it based on feedback. Procedures are strongest when they are shaped by real ministry experience rather than written in isolation.

Effective procedures share several common traits. They are clear, outlining steps in a logical, practical sequence. They are accessible, written in plain language, and easy to find when needed. They are also owned, assigned to a specific role or ministry, rather than existing as abstract instructions that no one feels responsible for following.

For example, consider a facility-use procedure. A clear procedure explains exactly how to submit a request, such as filling out an online form, and specifies the sequence:

- Step 1: Complete the form located on the church website.
- Step 2: Submit it to the church office.
- Step 3: The facilities coordinator reviews and approves requests within two business days.

Because the instructions are easy to understand and the form is available on the church website, the procedure is accessible. Assigning the facilities coordinator to manage requests and communicate approvals ensures the process is owned by a specific role, not left to anyone to handle.

Implementation often begins with a simple question: What does someone need to do first? From there, a strong procedure guides the reader through the process thoroughly without being overwhelming. When a procedure requires extensive explanation or constant clarification, it is usually trying to accomplish more than it should.

Most importantly, procedures should reflect real ministry workflows. If they are written without regard for how the church actually functions, frustration quickly follows, and compliance fades. The goal is not perfection. It is a consistent practice that supports people rather than burdening them.

Flexibility vs. Rigidity

One concern a leader may raise about procedures is that they will "tie our hands." That concern is understandable. Many leaders have encountered procedures that felt overly rigid or were enforced with little room for discernment. To overcome this resistance, it is important to openly acknowledge these concerns and create opportunities for input. For example, holding listening sessions allows leaders and teams to share their reservations and experiences, giving voice to any worries before new procedures are finalized. Inviting hesitant team members to participate in pilot programs gives them a chance to see how changes work in practice and to offer suggestions for improvement. Through this kind of engagement, leaders can move from skepticism to ownership, and practical feedback can shape stronger, more widely accepted procedures.

Procedures are not meant to suffocate ministry effectiveness. They are meant to steady it. They provide a normal way of operating so that not every situation requires reinventing the wheel. At the same time, they should leave room for pastoral wisdom. The important distinction is between what must remain firm and what can adapt.

Some standards are non-negotiable. Safety requirements, ethical boundaries, and legal obligations fall into this category. When it comes to protecting people or maintaining integrity, clarity matters more than flexibility.

Procedures supporting those standards should be direct and consistently followed.

Other processes, however, ought to acknowledge the realities of ministry. No two situations are exactly alike. Language such as "typically," "as appropriate," or "in consultation with" signals that leaders are expected to exercise judgment. Flexibility in these areas does not weaken a procedure. It recognizes that ministry involves people, and people rarely fit neatly into step-by-step formulas.

Overly rigid procedures often lead to workarounds. Flexible procedures create trust.

Ministry-Level Ownership

One of the most overlooked aspects of effective procedures is ownership. Procedures work best when they are written, maintained, and practiced at the ministry level, always within the boundaries established by policy.

Those entrusted with defining policy establish those boundaries. That responsibility matters. But ministry leaders are the ones closest to the daily realities of implementation. They understand the rhythms, pressures, and people involved in their specific areas of service. For that reason, they are often best equipped to develop procedures that reflect both the intent of the policy and the realities of the ministry.

This shared responsibility shields the church from two common pitfalls. It stops policy oversight from becoming micromanagement and ensures individual ministries stay aligned. Policies offer clarity and guidance, while procedures created by ministries add realism and sustainability.

Procedures imposed without input from the ministry often seem disconnected from the actual work and are often overlooked. When ministry leaders are involved in shaping procedures within established policies, participation improves because the process becomes more relevant and practical.

Ownership also includes responsibility for review and adjustment. As ministries grow or shift, procedures should evolve accordingly. Assigning procedural oversight to a role rather than a specific individual helps ensure continuity through staff transitions and leadership changes.

When ownership is unclear, procedures become fragile. People may assume someone else is responsible, or important practices may depend entirely on the memory of one person. Healthy procedures are connected to roles, communicated clearly, and reviewed regularly.

This intentional approach helps leaders delegate responsibility with confidence, knowing that procedures will be maintained and updated as the ministry evolves.

Case Study: When Procedures Are Missing

A church introduced a detailed facility-use policy that specified who could approve building requests and the conditions for approval. While the policy appeared solid on paper, there was no unified process for implementing it in reality. Requests were sent via text messages, hallway conversations, and occasional emails. Approval decisions varied depending on who was asked, and record-keeping was inconsistent.

For a season, this informality seemed manageable. Then a scheduling conflict arose between two ministry groups, and the disagreement quickly became public. Each group believed they had received proper approval. Each leader was convinced they had followed the policy. When the situation escalated to a church-wide conversation, it became clear that no one had violated authority. The real issue was that everyone had a slightly different understanding of how requests were handled.

The conflict revealed what had been absent all along: policies were in place, but clear procedures were not.

In response, the church developed simple, clearly defined procedures outlining how requests were to be submitted, how approvals were to be documented, and how communication would take place. The policy itself did not change. What changed was the consistency of its application. As a result, tension eased, misunderstandings decreased, and the facility-use process began functioning as intended.

Case Study: Flexibility That Builds Trust

Church leaders in one congregation kept running into the same challenge. Ministry rarely moved on a predictable schedule. Funerals came together on short notice. Community needs created unexpected opportunities. Volunteers sometimes stepped into roles quickly because someone else had to step away. The church had established policies and procedures, but the pace of ministry often created situations that did not fit neatly into the written process.

At first, some leaders believed the answer was simple: follow the procedures exactly as written. They wanted consistency, and their concern was understandable. But over time, volunteers began to feel slowed down rather than supported. What had been written to provide clarity started to feel like red tape. The frustration was not with the standards themselves. It was with the sense that there was no room for wisdom.

Instead of abandoning the procedures, the leadership team paused and asked a better question: How can we keep our standards while allowing appropriate discernment? They revised the procedures to include a clearly defined pathway for exceptions. The revision identified who could approve adjustments, when flexibility was appropriate, and which standards could not be set aside.

Nothing about the church's core commitments changed. Safety still mattered. Accountability still mattered. Communication still mattered. What changed was the way those commitments were applied in real ministry situations.

The difference was noticeable. Volunteers understood that expectations still mattered, but they also felt trusted to respond wisely when circumstances required judgment. Trust grew, not because procedures disappeared, but because the procedures finally reflected the pace and unpredictability of real ministry.

Conclusion

Procedures are where governance becomes tangible. They take policies off the page and into the rhythms of ordinary ministry. When written thoughtfully, they bring consistency without suffocating initiative and clarity without unnecessary restriction.

Churches that invest in sound procedures are not drifting toward bureaucracy. They recognize that ministry flourishes when people know what to expect. Clear procedures remove guesswork, protect volunteers, and steady leaders in moments of pressure. Instead of scrambling to figure things out in the middle of a crisis, the church can move forward with quiet confidence.

In the next chapter, we move from documents to direction. We will look at how churches evaluate their current governance practices and begin making changes carefully, patiently, and in ways that strengthen trust rather than disrupt it.

Reflection Questions

1. Where in our church do we have clear policies but inconsistent procedures? What evidence suggests that a gap exists?
2. Are our current procedures written at the right level of detail? Do they guide people clearly without overwhelming them?
3. Who "owns" each major area of procedure in our church? Is that ownership assigned to a role, or dependent on a specific person?
4. Have we clearly distinguished between non-negotiable standards and adaptable processes? Where might we be too rigid or too vague?
5. When procedures are not followed, is it usually because people are resistant or because the procedure does not reflect how the ministry actually functions?
6. If a new staff member or volunteer were to step into a key role tomorrow, would our written procedures help them succeed quickly?

7. What one procedural area, if clarified this year, would most increase trust and reduce confusion in our church?

Policy into Procedure Checklist

- Form a small team that includes those affected by the procedure.
- Review the relevant policy as a group.
- Identify and outline the key steps needed to put the policy into daily action.
- Draft the procedure in simple, clear language.
- Pilot the procedure in a limited setting and observe how it works.
- Gather feedback from those involved in using the procedure.
- Make necessary adjustments based on real-world experience and input.
- Finalize the procedure and implement it more broadly.

PART II
DIAGNOSIS AND CHANGE

CHAPTER 7

ASSESSING YOUR CURRENT GOVERNANCE

"Organizations need documents that define what it is and its mission and purpose, the structure by which it will do business, and the process that directs activity." Robert Welch[11]

Many pastors quietly recognize that something beneath the surface is not working as well as it should. Questions begin to form in the back of their minds. If we start revising our bylaws, what else will we need to change? If we create an employee policy manual, will it upset someone? If we begin requiring background checks, what might we discover?

Their concern is not whether governance issues exist but whether they are equipped to address them. Others worry that raising governance questions could reopen old conflicts or create new ones. For leaders already carrying heavy responsibilities, the thought of addressing governance can feel like pulling a thread that might unravel far more than expected.

The good news is that most governance challenges are more manageable than leaders initially fear. The difficulty is often not the size of the problem, but the uncertainty of where to begin. A careful review of one document, one process, or one recurring area of confusion can help leaders gain clarity and begin moving forward.

One difficulty is that governance is seldom obvious. When it is working well, it remains almost invisible. When it begins to falter, the symptoms usually appear somewhere else. Tension surfaces when expectations are unclear, misunderstandings recur, decisions feel harder than they should, or questions at business meetings leave leaders struggling to answer with confidence.

Before a church can improve its governance, it must first learn to see its situation clearly. This requires understanding the role each governance document plays, honestly reviewing existing structures, and identifying gaps or confusion. Some leaders may feel skeptical about this process, concerned that such evaluations could be disruptive or unnecessarily critical. However, this chapter is not about assigning blame or reopening old wounds. Rather, it is intended to help leaders evaluate their governance honestly, recognizing both strengths and weaknesses, and naming realities that may have gone unspoken for years.

Healthy churches proactively engage in conversations by cultivating the habit of stepping back, asking honest questions, and making thoughtful adjustments before minor issues escalate into bigger problems. They do not wait for conflict to trigger these discussions.

Where to Begin

Assessing governance begins with asking the right questions. Many churches start by asking whether they have the necessary documents. A more helpful question, however, is whether those documents are actually functioning as intended.

One simple place to start is by observing how often governing documents are used. When decisions are made, are the bylaws consulted? When questions arise, do leaders know where to look for guidance? Or are answers shaped mostly by memory, tradition, or whoever happens to be in the room at the time?

Another helpful step is to compare documents with daily practice. Many churches have governing documents that appear strong on paper but no longer reflect how the church actually operates. For example, a church's bylaws might state that all major ministry decisions require approval from a specific committee, but in practice, the senior pastor and a few long-time volunteers informally make these choices without any formal process. Over time, such informal habits replace formal structures, and leaders gradually stop noticing the difference.

Leaders should also examine the clarity of authority. Ask whether staff members, volunteers, and church leaders can clearly explain who has decision-making responsibility in different situations. If several people give different answers, the church likely has a governance clarity problem—even if written documents exist.

Self-evaluation works best when it includes voices from multiple levels of leadership. Pastors, staff, lay leaders, and long-serving members often experience governance differently. Listening to these perspectives helps reveal not only what the documents say, but how the church actually functions.

Healthy assessment is characterized by curiosity rather than defensiveness, supporting an environment where leaders are open to learning and improvement. This approach encourages honest reflection and constructive dialogue, making it more likely that underlying issues will be identified and addressed proactively. By embracing self-evaluation, churches can build a tradition of continuous growth, ensuring that their governance structures adapt to changing needs and better support their mission. Such assessments affirm that every church, regardless of its current health, possesses ongoing opportunities for development and enhanced effectiveness.

Identifying Shadow Governance

One of the most revealing parts of governance assessment is recognizing what might be called shadow governance. These are the informal systems that quietly operate alongside, or sometimes in place of, a church's formal authority structures.

Shadow governance rarely appears intentionally. It develops gradually. When governing documents are unclear, outdated, or rarely consulted, people naturally fill the gaps. A trusted staff member becomes the default decision maker. A committee continues operating long after its formal authority has ended. A long-time volunteer quietly controls access to information, resources, or approvals because that is how things have always worked.

At first, these arrangements often seem harmless, even helpful. Someone needed to act, and with no clear process in place, the church kept moving forward. Over time, however, these informal systems become normal. What began as a temporary solution slowly becomes an unwritten rule.

Eventually, leaders discover that decisions are no longer shaped primarily by the church's governing documents. Instead, they are influenced by personalities, habits, and long-standing expectations, creating informal centers of authority. This shift carries significant risks, as decision-making may become inconsistent, less transparent, and increasingly dependent on individual relationships or subjective preferences rather than established policy. As a result, authority persists, but it resides in places the church never intended to define, potentially undermining clarity, accountability, and fair governance.

The presence of shadow governance is not a moral failure. It is usually a sign that the church's formal governance system has not kept pace with the realities of ministry. When structures become unclear or outdated, informal authority almost always emerges to fill the space. Left unaddressed, shadow governance eventually creates confusion about who actually holds authority in the church.

Identifying shadow governance involves careful observation of decision-making processes. Listen for phrases such as, "That's just how we've always done it," or "You'll need to talk to her about that." Statements like these often reveal authority that exists outside the written structures of the church.

Shadow governance typically arises in situations that demand rapid or frequent decisions. Common examples include facility use, volunteer leadership, finances, scheduling, and crisis response. When formal procedures seem slow or unclear, informal ways of handling decisions often begin to emerge.

The longer these informal pathways remain unaddressed, the more difficult it becomes to restore clarity. For that reason, bringing shadow governance into the light is not about eliminating influence. Trusted relationships are one of the most valuable strengths a church can possess. Healthy churches will always rely on trusted people, and effective governance can recognize and formalize these relationships so that personal trust is honored, rather than undermined, by the structures that support ministry. The goal is to ensure that influence operates within structures that provide clarity, accountability, and shared understanding.

Where Churches Think They're Fine

One of the most difficult parts of governance assessment is recognizing the areas where a church assumes everything is healthy. In many cases, the systems feel fine because nothing obvious has gone wrong.

Finances are stable. Attendance is steady. Conflict is minimal. These are encouraging signs, but they are not always reliable indicators of governance health. Governance systems are rarely tested during seasons of stability. They are tested when leadership changes, when pressure increases, or when disagreement arises.

Churches also tend to measure governance health by the level of trust among leaders. Trust is a tremendous gift, but it is not a substitute for clarity. In fact, high trust can sometimes hide weaknesses. Informal systems may work well while relationships are strong, but when trust is strained, those same systems can quickly create confusion.

Longevity can also create a blind spot. Practices that have existed for many years begin to feel legitimate simply because they have been around for so long. Yet age alone does not establish authority. When practices are not documented or formally approved, they depend heavily on the continuity of people rather than the continuity of the process.

Finally, many churches assume they are fine because change feels risky. Revisiting governing documents can seem disruptive, particularly in churches that value harmony. Yet avoiding assessment in order to preserve peace often delays conflict rather than preventing it.

Governance assessment is not about fixing something that is broken. It is about strengthening what may be fragile before it is tested.

Signs That A Governance Assessment Is Needed

While every church benefits from regular governance assessments, some indicators suggest that a more careful review might be needed. These signs rarely occur simultaneously. More often, they tend to appear gradually, emerging subtly in the church's everyday operations.

Frequent confusion about authority is one of the clearest indicators. When leaders regularly ask who has the authority to approve something, governance clarity is lacking. Inconsistency can also reveal a problem. If similar situations are handled differently depending on who is involved, the church's policies or procedures may be unclear, incomplete, or not used at all.

Resistance to change may also signal underlying strain in governance. When proposed adjustments trigger disproportionate fear or suspicion, it may be because authority structures are unclear or mistrusted. In some cases, staff or volunteer burnout can also point to governance issues. When expectations are undefined, decisions remain unresolved, or accountability is uneven, people often carry emotional weight that healthy systems should help distribute. Leaders can create structured opportunities for feedback through listening sessions, advance-submitted written questions, or conversations with ministry teams. The goal is not to collect complaints, but to understand where confusion or concern may already exist. Additionally, leaders may find it helpful to share stories of positive change from other contexts that show how thoughtful adjustments have supported ministry goals and created lasting benefits. Taking these steps builds trust and helps those who feel hesitant to participate in constructive conversations about governance.

Recognizing these signals early allows churches to respond thoughtfully rather than reactively.

Creating a Safe Assessment Environment

Governance assessment should also ask a simple but important question: Who owns this responsibility?

In many churches, responsibilities are attached more to personalities than to roles. A long-time staff member knows how a process works. A committee chair understands the history behind a decision. A trusted volunteer handles a ministry detail because they have always handled it. While this may work for a season, it becomes fragile when that person steps away, changes roles, or becomes unavailable.

Healthy governance assigns responsibility to roles rather than personalities. This does not remove the value of faithful people. It protects the church by ensuring that important responsibilities do not disappear when individuals transition.

Ownership should be clear enough that a new leader can understand who is responsible, who has authority, and where to find the process. When ownership is unclear, confusion grows quickly. People may assume someone else is handling a matter, or several people may act independently without realizing their responsibilities overlap.

Clarifying ownership is one of the most practical outcomes of governance assessment. It helps the church move from informal dependence to shared understanding. When responsibility is connected to a defined role, the church is better prepared for leadership transitions, ministry growth, and unexpected challenges.

Ownership Gap Checklist

- What responsibility or process is being evaluated?
- Who currently handles it?
- Is that responsibility assigned to a role or dependent on a person?
- Who has the authority to make the decision?
- Who should be consulted before action is taken?
- Who should be informed after the decision is made?
- Where is this responsibility written down?
- Are there gaps, overlaps, or assumptions?
- If the current person stepped away, would the process still continue clearly?
- What needs to be clarified, documented, or reassigned?

Conclusion

Assessing governance requires a measure of leadership courage. It takes humility to acknowledge where systems are unclear and wisdom to address those gaps before they grow into larger problems.

Healthy churches understand that governance assessment is not a criticism but a form of stewardship. When leaders take the time to examine their structures honestly, they create space for clearer expectations, healthier transitions, and stronger unity. Instead of relying on assumptions or long-standing habits, they move toward intentional systems that support the church's mission.

Governance rarely improves by accident. It improves when leaders are willing to pause, ask honest questions, and make thoughtful adjustments.

In the next chapter, we will examine how churches transition from assessment to action, focusing on planning governance improvements that respect culture, maintain trust, and enhance the church's strength for the future.

Reflection Questions for Leadership Teams

1. When was the last time your church intentionally reviewed its governing documents?
2. Are they regularly referenced when decisions are made, or do leaders rely primarily on memory, tradition, or past practice?
3. Would different leaders in your church give the same answer about who has authority in common situations? If answers vary, what areas of governance may require explanation?
4. Where do decisions actually happen in your church?
5. Do those decision points match what your bylaws, policies, or procedures describe?
6. Are there areas where informal influence carries more authority than written structures?
7. What examples of shadow governance might exist in your ministry context?
8. Have long-standing practices quietly replaced written processes?
9. Are there habits or traditions that function like policy even though they have never been formally adopted?
10. Which areas of church life seem to generate the most confusion or repeated questions?

11. What might those patterns reveal about gaps in governance clarity?
12. If a new staff member or ministry leader joined your church tomorrow, would your governance documents help them understand how decisions are made?

CHAPTER 8

PLANNING FOR CHANGE: WHAT WILL IT TAKE?

After a church objectively evaluates its current governance, the next logical question is: How should we address what we have discovered?

Many well-intentioned efforts stall at this point. Leaders see the gaps, acknowledge the risks, and agree that improvements are necessary, but they often struggle to move forward. The obstacle is rarely a lack of information. More often, it is uncertainty about how to begin and what the process might entail. To move from awareness to action, leaders can take a simple yet practical first step, such as forming a small task force to explore the issues identified or hosting a listening session to gather input from key stakeholders. These initial actions provide a concrete starting point for progress, foster shared ownership, and help clarify the path forward.

Governance change is not simply a technical exercise. It is also a cultural one. While documents can be rewritten quickly, trust, understanding, and shared expectations tend to develop more gradually. Effective change planning demands careful consideration of culture, sequence, and leadership credibility. Churches that ignore these factors might implement new documents without gaining the clarity they were designed to deliver.

Culture Eats Governance for Breakfast

It is often attributed to Peter Drucker that the phrase "culture eats strategy for breakfast" meaning that "no matter how great your business strategy is, your plan will fail without a company culture that encourages people to implement it."."[12] That same concept applies to church governance. The idea that "church culture eats governance for breakfast" illustrates a hard truth: even the most well-designed governance documents can be undermined by a resistant or misaligned culture. Churches do not adopt governance changes in isolation. These changes occur within complex relational systems shaped by history, trust, fears, and expectations. Long before a document is consulted, culture has already answered certain questions. Who is listened to? What happens when someone disagrees? How are mistakes handled? These unwritten norms often determine whether new governance structures will be embraced or quietly ignored.

Churches with strong relational cultures but weak governance often rely on goodwill to compensate for unclear systems. For a time, this can work. When people trust one another, many decisions happen smoothly, even when processes are undefined. But as ministries grow, leadership transitions occur, and decisions become more complex, goodwill alone eventually becomes insufficient.

At the same time, churches that attempt to implement governance changes without recognizing their relational culture often encounter resistance. Even when the proposed changes are wise and necessary, they can feel disruptive if they appear disconnected from the church's shared history and values. When members sense that governance changes are being introduced without understanding the church's culture, trust can erode quickly.

For this reason, effective planning begins with an honest awareness of the church's culture. Leaders should ask questions such as:

- How does this church typically respond when change is introduced?
- Where is trust strong, and where might it be fragile?
- What stories or past experiences shape how people view leadership and authority?

Governance changes that align with a church's culture are far more likely to take root. Changes that ignore cultural realities may pass on paper, but they rarely produce lasting clarity or sustained change.

Sequencing Change: Where to Start

One of the most common mistakes churches make is trying to change everything at once. When leaders recognize governance gaps, the natural instinct is to fix every problem immediately. While the motivation is understandable, this approach often overwhelms people and unintentionally erodes trust.

Healthy change usually happens step by step. Some decisions create the conditions for others, which is why clarity must come before complexity.

In many churches, the first step is clarifying authority. Before policies or procedures are revised, leaders need to ensure that the church's governing documents, typically the constitution and bylaws, clearly define who has the authority to make, approve, or amend those changes. When this foundation is unclear, even well-intentioned improvements can create confusion or conflict because people are unsure who is responsible for the decision.

Once authority is clearly established in the governing documents, the next step is to align those documents. Churches should address foundational inconsistencies, such as conflicting bylaws, outdated provisions, or unclear responsibilities, before adding new layers of policy. Adding policies on top of unclear governance is like building on uneven ground.

Only after authority and alignment are addressed should churches begin to expand their policies and procedures. When change follows this progression, leaders can explain not only what is changing but also why the change fits within a clear and orderly framework.

Effective sequencing also requires thoughtful communication. People need time to understand new ideas, ask questions, and adjust their expectations. When change happens too quickly, even positive improvements can create suspicion simply because people feel rushed.

Effective sequencing also requires thoughtful communication. People need time to understand new ideas, ask questions, and adjust their expectations. When change happens too quickly, even positive improvements can create suspicion simply because people feel rushed.

To help leaders communicate effectively, it can be useful to offer clear, reassuring phrases when presenting governance changes to the congregation. For example, consider statements such as:

- "We want to keep what is healthy and valued in our church while also preparing for the future."
- "Your input and questions are welcome as we consider these changes together."

- "These updates are meant to support our ministry, not to replace our church's unique identity."
- "We are committed to moving at a pace where everyone can understand and participate."

Simple, thoughtful language like this can reduce anxiety, build trust, and help members see that the goal of governance change is clarity and unity within the church family.

Sequencing change is not about slowing momentum. It is about ensuring that the progress a church makes today will still make sense tomorrow.

Why Leadership Credibility Is Required

Leadership credibility is one of the most overlooked elements of governance change. Documents do not implement themselves. Before people follow policies or procedures, they decide whether they trust the leaders asking them to do so.

Credibility is built through consistency, transparency, and humility. Leaders who ask others to follow governance structures must also demonstrate their own willingness to be guided by them. Nothing damages credibility faster than leaders who treat governing documents as tools for others while making exceptions for themselves.

Credibility also depends on how leaders explain the need for change. Governance improvements often raise an unspoken question among church members: *Why are we addressing this now?* If leaders speak carelessly, the conversation can quickly feel like criticism of the church's past or of previous leaders.[13]

Wise leaders approach this moment carefully. Rather than framing change as correcting past failures, they present it as strengthening the church for the future. Churches grow, ministries expand, and leadership responsibilities become more complex over time. Governance systems that once worked informally may simply need greater clarity as the church matures.

For long-tenured pastors, this requires humility. People may wonder why certain changes were not addressed earlier. A healthy response does not assign blame or defensiveness. Instead, it acknowledges that churches grow and learn over time. Saying something as simple as *"As our church has grown, we are realizing we need clearer structures to support the ministry God has given us"* often communicates far more trust than trying to justify the timing.

For newer pastors, the temptation can be different. It can be easy to attribute governance gaps to previous leadership. Yet casting vision by criticizing the past rarely builds trust. Healthy leadership honors the church's history while helping the congregation prepare for the future.

Shared ownership also strengthens credibility. Governance changes that appear purely top-down can feel threatening, even when they are wise. Inviting lay leaders, staff members, or advisory groups into the process helps people see that the goal is not control but clarity. Within the proper authority structures, collaborative planning often leads to stronger solutions and broader trust.

Finally, leaders must be prepared to persist. Governance changes rarely generate immediate enthusiasm. They often raise questions, confusion, or nostalgia for how things were done before. Leaders with credibility respond patiently rather than defensively and remain steady as people adjust.

Without credibility, governance changes may pass a vote but rarely transform how the church actually functions.

Communicating Change Clearly

Clear communication is essential when churches begin making governance changes. Most resistance to change does not come from hostility but from uncertainty. When people do not understand what is happening, they naturally fill the gaps with assumptions.

Church members often worry about losing influence, being excluded from decisions, or seeing traditions they value disappear. Because of this, leaders should communicate not only what is changing but also what is not changing. Reassurance matters, especially in churches where trust and relationships carry deep history.

Leaders should also recognize that governance changes rarely fail because the ideas themselves are wrong. More often, they struggle because the changes were introduced faster than the church could understand them. Good communication slows the process enough for people to see how the changes support the mission of the church rather than threaten it.

Healthy communication also creates space for questions. Not every concern signals opposition. Many questions simply reflect a sincere desire to understand how new structures will affect the life of the church. Leaders who listen patiently often discover that concerns fade once people feel listened to and informed.

In practice, this often means communicating changes in stages. Leaders may first explain the reason for the proposed change and clearly describe what is being addressed. The proposed changes can then be shared with the congregation before any vote takes place. Allowing time between the presentation of a proposal and a formal decision gives people space to reflect, ask questions, and understand how the change fits into the church's broader mission.

It is also wise to address changes one step at a time. When multiple adjustments are needed, introducing them gradually helps the church focus on each issue without feeling overwhelmed. If a particular proposal creates confusion or concern, leaders can pause that discussion and return to it later while continuing progress in other areas.

At the same time, leaders must recognize that some resistance may come from informal authority structures that developed over time. When governance becomes clearer, those who benefited from ambiguity may feel uncomfortable. Responding to these situations requires calm, steady leadership rather than defensiveness.

When churches communicate governance changes clearly and patiently, people are far more likely to see those changes not as threats but as steps toward greater clarity, stewardship, and unity.

Measuring Readiness, Not Just Desire

Many churches desire change. Far fewer are ready for it.

Readiness involves more than agreeing that something should improve. It includes emotional capacity, relational trust, and, crucially, alignment among the leadership on the purpose and approach to change. Leadership alignment is a foundational prerequisite because, without a shared commitment among key leaders, efforts toward governance improvement can easily stall or lead to confusion. A church may recognize that its governance needs strengthening but still lacks the stability needed to engage the process effectively.

Leaders should pause long enough to ask whether the church has the margin to do this work thoughtfully. Are the key leaders unified about the proposed direction? Is the church in a season where people can absorb change, or are they already carrying the weight of other transitions? Governance work requires patience, attention, and trust.

Sometimes, the most faithful approach is to focus on preparation rather than rushing into action. Churches often need time to build stronger ties among leaders, work through ongoing conflicts, or clarify expectations before making major structural changes. Taking this time helps create a more united and confident community as they move forward. Addressing these relational foundations first generally leads to more effective governance improvements later.

A church that moves too quickly may adopt better documents but lose the trust needed to use them well.

Readiness also means that leaders are prepared to walk patiently with the congregation through the process. Governance change is rarely a single decision. It is a season of learning, conversation, and adjustment.

Thoughtful planning respects the individuals affected by new systems. When leaders assess readiness with the same rigor as desire, they set the stage for sustainable change within the church.

Conclusion

Planning for governance change is not simply about drafting better documents. It is about preparing hearts, structures, and expectations within the life of the church.

Culture shapes how we see change, and the way we sequence efforts can really make a difference in keeping changes lasting. When leaders are credible, it builds trust in these initiatives. Overlooking these important factors might make it harder for governance changes to truly take hold. Recognizing and embracing these elements can help ensure a smoother and more successful transformation.

Wise leaders avoid rushing to clarity or insisting on immediate compliance. Instead, they lead with patience, communicate openly, and nurture trust thoughtfully. They understand that governance change involves not just structural adjustments, but also building relationships.

When handled thoughtfully, governance can be a blessing to the church. It establishes clarity in place of confusion and stability in the midst of uncertainty. Over time, these frameworks help leaders and congregations shift their focus from managing internal issues to actively pursuing the mission God has entrusted to them.

In the next chapter, we will discuss how churches can manage governance changes smoothly by engaging members thoughtfully, addressing tensions promptly, and maintaining unity during transitions.

Reflection Questions

1. How does our church typically respond to change?
2. Do our leaders share a clear understanding of how governance decisions are made?
3. Where might informal systems be carrying more influence than our written structures?
4. How much trust currently exists among our leadership and congregation?
5. Are we trying to solve too many governance issues at once?
6. How clearly could we explain the purpose of governance improvements to our congregation?
7. Is our church ready for governance change, or do we first need to strengthen trust, communication, or leadership alignment?

CHAPTER 9

AVOIDING UNNECESSARY CONFLICT

"When the church lives in harmony and agreement, it can be a visual testimony in the world that rarely sees such a thing in our divisive and polarized society." Dean Inserra[14]

Conflict within the church is not necessarily a sign of failure; often, it arises naturally from growth and change. The Bible itself recognizes this, as seen in Acts 6, where early church conflicts over the distribution of resources led to the appointment of new leaders. Likewise, Acts 15 records a significant disagreement among church leaders over whether to include Gentile believers. These instances remind us that conflict has been a consistent part of church life and can provide opportunities for growth and understanding. However, much church conflict is unnecessary, usually caused not by difficult individuals but by unclear authority, mismatched expectations, or broken communication.

Good governance cannot eliminate disagreement, and it should not try to. Healthy churches will always wrestle with important decisions. What good governance can do is reduce confusion. Dr. Jody Dean wrote, "The overall process for leadership and guiding documents is intended to help a church navigate conflict and conduct business legally and ethically."[15] When people understand who has responsibility for decisions, how those decisions are made, and how concerns can be raised, tension loses much of its destructive power.

This chapter first examines the types of conflict that clear governance can prevent, then explores practical strategies churches can adopt to respond wisely when tensions emerge.

Why Conflict Happens in Churches

Conflict in churches rarely originates at the surface level, where it is most visible. While disagreements may appear to be interpersonal, they often stem from deeper systemic issues such as unclear expectations, ambiguous delineations of authority, or unrealistic assumptions about roles and responsibilities. These underlying factors foster an environment where misunderstandings are more likely, acting as the true root causes of many conflicts.

When authority is not clearly defined, it is inevitably assumed. Different people assume different things, and those assumptions eventually collide. Conflict follows, not because someone acted maliciously, but because expectations were never aligned.

Healthy churches clarify decision-making processes and responsibilities. This clarity starts with governing documents such as constitutions and bylaws, but it must extend beyond written rules. Authority should also be well understood, clearly communicated, and consistently applied.

Churches should be able to answer basic questions with confidence:

- Who has responsibility for this decision?
- Who should be consulted before it is made?
- Who should be informed after it is made?
- What process exists if someone disagrees?

When these answers vary depending on who is asked, conflict becomes almost inevitable.

Clear authority does not mean centralized control. In fact, healthy governance often distributes responsibility broadly. But delegation without definition leads to frustration. When roles and responsibilities are understood, leaders can act with confidence and members can understand how decisions were reached, even when they disagree with the outcome.

Perhaps most importantly, clarity protects relationships. People are far less likely to take decisions personally when they understand the process behind them.

When Conflict Is Actually a Governance Problem

One of the most freeing insights for church leaders is realizing that some conflict is structural rather than personal. When the same disagreements repeatedly come up, especially around authority, approval, or decision boundaries, the issue might not be in the personalities involved. Instead, it could stem from the governance system itself. If the structure is unclear, people will try to fill in the gaps. Some leaders take on responsibilities that were never officially assigned. Others hesitate to act because they fear overstepping their role. Still, some turn to tradition or relational influence when formal processes seem lacking.

Addressing the people involved without addressing the structure rarely solves the issue. It simply postpones the next conflict.

Structural conflict calls for structural solutions. Clarifying governing documents, aligning policies with authority, and creating clear processes often resolve tensions that pastoral counseling alone cannot address.

This does not minimize the importance of relational care. It strengthens it. When leaders address the underlying systems that produce confusion, they reduce emotional strain across the church and create space for healthier relationships.

Tensions Churches Must Learn to Manage

Even with clear governance, certain tensions are unavoidable in church life. Avoiding unnecessary conflict does not mean eliminating tension. It means learning to manage it faithfully.

In fact, tension often accompanies healthy change. Growth brings tension. Revitalization brings tension. Even faithful obedience to a new direction can create discomfort as people adjust to new expectations. Leaders should not interpret every moment of tension as failure. Often, it is simply evidence that a church is moving.

For this reason, a church's capacity for change is closely tied to its capacity to handle tension. Leaders who expect tension are better prepared to guide a church through it. When leaders recognize tension as a normal part of growth, they can respond with steadiness rather than anxiety.

Moments of tension are not leadership failures; they are leadership moments. They invite leaders to clarify direction, strengthen trust, and guide people through uncertainty. Churches rarely grow without some measure of tension, but wise leadership ensures that tension becomes a pathway to clarity rather than a cause of division.

One common tension exists between pastoral care and organizational clarity. Churches rightly prioritize compassion and flexibility. However, when exceptions become the norm, policies lose credibility and people begin to question fairness. Leaders must balance sensitivity to individual situations with the consistency needed to preserve the integrity of the church's systems.

Another tension often emerges between long-standing members and newer leaders. Long-term members carry deep relational investment and institutional memory. Newer leaders may bring fresh clarity and structural improvements. Conflict arises when either side feels dismissed. Healthy governance honors both experience and responsibility.

Churches often balance between pursuing a vision and maintaining stability. While vision initiatives can energize a congregation, they can cause confusion if governance structures are unclear. Conversely, excessively rigid systems may hinder healthy innovation. Effective leadership guides the vision to progress within well-defined authority frameworks.

Many churches experience tension between informal influence and formal authority. Trusted individuals often hold significant relational influence without clearly defined responsibility. When governance structures formalize authority, those individuals may feel displaced even when no harm is intended. Recognizing this dynamic allows leaders to address it with empathy rather than surprise.

These tensions are not problems to eliminate. They are realities that faithful leadership must steward with patience, clarity, and grace.

Communicating in Ways That Reduce Conflict

Clear governance depends on clear communication. Many conflicts that appear to be disagreements are actually misunderstandings. For example, if church leaders decide to change the schedule of a longstanding event but do not communicate the reasons behind this decision, members may assume the event is being deprioritized or that their input was not valued. When people do not fully understand what is happening or why a decision was made, they naturally fill the gaps with assumptions.

One of the most helpful communication practices is explaining the "why" before the "what." When leaders announce decisions without context, people are left to interpret the decision on their own. Explaining the reasoning behind a governance decision helps people understand the broader purpose, even when they may not personally agree with the outcome.

It can also be helpful to name the decision-making process itself. Statements such as, "This decision follows the direction established in our bylaws," or "This policy guides how we handle situations like this," help shift the focus away from personalities and toward shared principles. When people understand the process, decisions feel less personal and more consistent.

Consistency among leaders is equally important. When different leaders offer different explanations or communicate with different tones, confusion grows quickly. Alignment among pastoral staff, key lay leaders, and ministry teams strengthens trust because the church hears a unified message.

Churches should also provide clear pathways for feedback. When people do not know how to ask questions or express concerns, frustration often surfaces in unhelpful ways. A healthy feedback process does not guarantee agreement, but it offers a constructive space for concerns to be heard. Churches may use listening sessions, written questions, scheduled conversations, or other appropriate methods. The method matters less than the clarity of the pathway and the willingness of leaders to listen carefully.

Leaders should also remember that communication is not only verbal. Timing, follow-through, and consistency communicate just as strongly as words. A policy that is explained clearly but applied inconsistently can create more confusion than one that was simply communicated poorly.

Good communication does not eliminate every disagreement, but it often prevents conflict from escalating unnecessarily. When people understand how a decision was made, they are far more willing to accept an outcome they might not have chosen themselves.

Handling Hard Conversations Faithfully

Avoiding unnecessary conflict does not mean avoiding difficult conversations. In fact, avoiding clarity often creates deeper division later.

Unity is not the same as uniformity, and peace is not the same as silence. Biblical unity grows from shared purpose, mutual submission, and honest engagement. Scripture repeatedly calls believers to speak truthfully with one another in love (Ephesians 4:15, 25). Governance supports that kind of unity by establishing shared expectations and fair processes for addressing concerns.

Leaders should resist the temptation to preserve superficial harmony at the expense of long-term health. When concerns remain unspoken or authority remains unclear, tension simply builds beneath the surface until it eventually emerges in more damaging ways.

Wise leaders approach difficult conversations with humility and clarity. They listen carefully before responding, seek to understand concerns rather than dismiss them, and keep the conversation anchored to shared principles rather than personal preferences. Often, the most important step is simply creating a space where questions can be asked honestly and addressed respectfully.

Clear governance allows churches to disagree without dividing because the boundaries and processes for those disagreements are understood. When people know how concerns will be handled and who carries responsibility for decisions, disagreements are less likely to become personal conflicts.

When conflict arises, leaders should model calm, humility, and faithfulness to established processes. How leaders respond to tension teaches the congregation to trust governance structures.

Handled wisely, even difficult conversations can strengthen unity. They remind the church that truth and grace belong together and that healthy governance provides a framework in which both can flourish.

Preparing for Difficult Situations Before They Arise

Church leaders hope they never face a truly difficult or disruptive situation within the congregation. Yet experience shows that most churches will eventually encounter moments that test their leadership, unity, and clarity.

In those moments, the strength of a church's governance becomes clear.

Kenneth Haugk noted that "an ounce of prevention now is worth much more than a pound of damage control."[16] That prevention does not happen in the moment of conflict. It is built over time through clear processes, consistent practices, and well-trained leadership.

Situations that create tension or division often do not begin with an obvious disruption. They begin in areas where expectations are unclear, processes are inconsistent, or authority is poorly understood. When those gaps exist, they can be exploited, intentionally or unintentionally, to create confusion and strain.

For that reason, church leaders must regularly examine their systems. Governance is not only about guiding a healthy ministry. It also protects the church when challenges arise. Clear bylaws, personnel policies, financial accountability practices, facility use procedures, and child protection policies all help establish stability.

These systems may feel tedious at times, but they serve an important purpose. As Haugk observed, procedures often seem inconvenient until they are needed. When followed consistently, they serve as safeguards that prevent situations from escalating unnecessarily.[17]

Preparation also includes leadership awareness. Churches benefit when leaders are equipped to recognize early signs of tension, respond wisely, and avoid unintentionally creating opportunities for conflict to grow.

Educating leadership teams in these areas strengthens the church's ability to respond calmly and faithfully when challenges arise.

At times, leaders may already be aware of individuals who tend to create tension within the church. In those situations, wisdom and care are essential. Haugk advises that such situations must be handled "very, very carefully." Leaders should remain kind, consistent, and grounded in established processes, while avoiding unnecessary escalation or informal handling of sensitive situations.

As legendary UCLA basketball coach John Wooden is known for saying, "the time to prepare is not after you have been given the opportunity. It is long before that opportunity arises."[18] The same is true in church leadership. Churches that prepare in advance are far better equipped to navigate difficult moments without losing clarity or unity.

Conclusion

Unnecessary conflict thrives in environments of ambiguity, assumption, and inconsistent communication. When authority is unclear and expectations remain unstated, disagreements easily become personal and emotionally charged.

Effective governance does not eliminate disagreement, nor should it. Healthy churches will inevitably face difficult decisions. Governance clarifies the process by shifting conflicts from personal disputes to procedural debates and from emotional responses to deliberate conversations. Clear governance is not only a practical necessity but also an expression of the church's calling to be a community shaped by the character of Christ. When decision-making reflects order, fairness, transparency, and respect, it embodies biblical principles and serves the church's mission. In this way, governance supports the church in pursuing unity, justice, and a shared purpose for the sake of its gospel witness.

Leaders must also recognize that tension often accompanies growth and change. The goal is not to remove tension entirely but to guide it wisely. Churches that learn to steward tension rather than fear it are better prepared to navigate seasons of transition and revitalization.

Effective communication and strong leadership are key to encouraging positive engagement with disagreements. Leaders who clearly explain their reasoning, promote open dialogue, and show humility in difficult conversations foster mutual understanding and set a healthy example for handling conflicts. Combining transparent communication with principled leadership helps the church navigate disagreements in ways that protect relationships and build trust within the community.

Churches that prioritize clarity of authority, manage tension intentionally, and communicate transparently create space for healthy disagreement without fracture. In doing so, they protect unity not by avoiding conflict but by stewarding it faithfully.

In this way, governance becomes not a source of division but a tool that helps the church pursue its mission with clarity, trust, and unity.

Reflection Questions

1. When conflict arises in our church, do we tend to treat it as a personal disagreement, or do we pause to ask

whether it may be rooted in unclear systems or expectations?

2. Are decision-making responsibilities in our church clearly understood, or do people often disagree about who has the authority to make certain decisions?
3. How well does our church handle tension during seasons of change? Do leaders and members expect some tension, or do we tend to interpret tension as failure?
4. When leaders communicate decisions, do we typically explain why the decision was made, or do people mostly hear the decision itself without context?
5. Are there clear, healthy pathways for members to ask questions or express concerns, or do frustrations tend to surface informally in side conversations?
6. How do leaders in our church model responses to conflict? Do we demonstrate calm, humility, and faithfulness to process, or do tensions tend to escalate quickly?
7. Looking ahead, what one area of clarity in our church's governance could most reduce unnecessary conflict?
8. What kind of culture does our church currently have when conflict arises? What would it take to move toward healthier engagement?

PART III
SUSTAINING HEALTH

CHAPTER 10

IMPLEMENTING GOVERNANCE IN REAL CHURCH LIFE

"Churches, seminaries, and nonprofit organizations are notorious for saying they need change and then resisting the very leader they called to bring it." Tod Bolsinger[19]

Revising governance documents can feel like a major accomplishment. Committees have met, language has been refined, and votes have been taken. For many churches, adopting new bylaws or policies feels like the finish line, when in reality it is only the beginning.

Governance strengthens a church only when it moves from paper to practice.

Written documents can clarify authority and expectations, but they cannot shape culture on their own. If governing structures are not understood, taught, and consistently practiced, even well-written documents eventually drift into obscurity. Over time, habits quietly return to what they were before, and the clarity the church worked so hard to establish begins to fade.

Scripture reminds us that faithful ministry is not only about good intentions, but about ordered and thoughtful practice. Writing to the Corinthian church, the Apostle Paul shared a straightforward principle applicable to the church.

"But all things should be done decently and in order." 1 Corinthians 14:40

Paul's instruction was not about bureaucracy or control. It was about protecting the church from confusion so that the work of the gospel could move forward with clarity and unity. Order in the church serves the mission of the church.

The same principle applies to governance. Churches may create and adopt good documents, but unless those structures are integrated into daily leadership and ministry, they remain little more than words on paper.

The previous chapters have focused on building and clarifying governance. We explored the biblical foundations of order and stewardship, examined the roles of constitutions, bylaws, policies, and procedures, and considered how churches can assess and improve their governance systems. Those steps are essential, but they do not complete the work.

Healthy governance must be sustained.

The chapters that follow examine how churches can maintain clarity in governance over time. They explore how governing structures become part of everyday ministry practice, how churches wisely steward legal and organizational risks, and how governance systems can be developed to strengthen the church across generations of leadership.

The goal is not simply to produce better documents.

The goal is to cultivate healthier churches.

Moving From Paper to Practice

Documents do not change churches. Leaders do.

Governance documents offer clarity, but they alone do not shape a church's life. It is up to leadership to decide whether these structures become part of daily ministry or stay just words on paper.

Many churches invest significant time revising governance documents. Committees meet, language is refined, and congregations vote to approve the changes. In the moment, adopting new bylaws or policies can feel like completing an important task. Yet churches often find that daily ministry habits remain largely unchanged.

The reason is simple: governance documents clarify expectations, but they do not automatically shape behavior.

Without intentional implementation, new policies and structures gradually become background information rather than serving as guiding frameworks. Leaders continue to operate according to typical patterns, and the clarity the church worked hard to establish slowly fades from everyday practice.

Effective governance requires more than well-crafted documents; it depends on leaders who consistently adhere to the frameworks those documents outline. The process begins with leadership alignment. Pastors, staff, and lay leaders need to understand not only the content of the governance documents but also the purpose behind those structures. Building this alignment is intentional. Churches can promote shared understanding through methods such as facilitated group discussions that encourage open dialogue about governance principles, shared devotional times focused on the biblical foundations of order and leadership, or leadership training sessions that use real-life scenarios to illustrate how decisions should be made. When leaders engage in these practices together, they foster unity, clarify expectations, and develop a sense of collective responsibility. As a result, when leaders share a common understanding of governance principles, they are better able to apply them consistently in their daily decision-making.

Leadership alignment is best built through intentional practices. Churches can set aside time for annual retreats or governance-focused workshops, where leaders collaboratively discuss and clarify roles, responsibilities, and decision-making processes. Regular leadership meetings can also include a standing agenda item to review policy updates, discuss real-life scenarios, and ensure everyone shares a common understanding. Occasional team-building activities or facilitated discussions provide a safe space for leaders to surface questions or concerns, strengthening both relationships and shared clarity. By making alignment an ongoing priority, churches foster a leadership culture in which good governance becomes second nature.

Implementation also depends on deliberate reference. Governance documents should not be kept in a binder or digital folder that only a few people review. When questions arise, leaders should consult the church's bylaws, policies, or procedures to guide their decisions. For example, during leadership meetings, teams can refer to the bylaws to clarify who has the authority to approve a new ministry initiative. When resolving a disagreement about the use of church facilities, leaders might consult the facilities policy to ensure their approach corresponds with established guidelines. If a difficult personnel issue emerges, the team can review procedures for staff evaluations or conflict resolution before making decisions. Over time, these habits emphasize the importance of those documents in shaping the church's shared life.

Finally, governance becomes sustainable when leaders model the structures they want others to follow. Churches rarely function solely through documents; they follow the example set by their leaders. When leaders show respect for the church's governance systems, the congregation learns to trust and follow their lead.

Governance becomes culture when leaders consistently practice what the documents describe.

Teaching Governance to the Church

Many church leaders assume members understand how church governance works. Because leaders regularly interact with governing documents, it is easy to assume others are familiar with them as well. In reality, most members have limited exposure to the church's governance structures and rarely think about them.

This is why church governance must be intentionally taught.

When governance is left unspoken, members often fill the gaps with assumptions. They depend on past experiences, informal traditions, or what they believe churches usually do. Over time, these assumptions can create confusion about how decisions are made, who has the authority to act, and how concerns should be handled.

Leadership transitions provide one of the most important opportunities for governance instruction. When new staff members, ministry leaders, or volunteer leaders begin serving, they should receive clear guidance about how the church's governing structures function. Understanding how authority flows within the church helps leaders serve with confidence and reduces misunderstandings later.

Church leadership groups also benefit from periodic governance review. Deacons, elders, committee members, and ministry team leaders often carry significant responsibility within the life of the church. Taking time to revisit governing documents with these leaders helps ensure that everyone is working from the same understanding of the church's structures and expectations.

Membership processes present another important opportunity. New member classes usually concentrate on doctrine, mission, and church culture. Including a brief explanation of how the church makes decisions, how authority is structured, and how members participate in that process helps build trust and transparency from the beginning.

In many churches, governance education happens through simple, consistent practices such as:

- Leadership orientation for new staff and ministry leaders
- Periodic review with deacons, elders, or ministry leadership teams
- A brief governance overview in new member classes
- Short explanations during business meetings when decisions are presented

These moments do not require lengthy lectures or technical explanations. Most members simply need to understand the basic principles that guide the church's life together. When those principles are explained clearly and consistently, the congregation is far more likely to trust the decisions made within that framework.

To make these principles accessible, leaders can use simple teaching methods, such as sharing real-life stories that illustrate governance in action. Brief Q&A sessions during meetings allow members to ask questions and clarify how decisions are made. Leaders might also provide short, scenario-based examples or include visual aids like flowcharts to show how decisions move through the church's structure. These approaches help demystify governance and equip members to participate confidently, without overwhelming them with too much detail.

Governance is not simply written. It must be taught.

Aligning Vision With Governance

Mission and vision play distinct roles in a church's life. Though the two terms are often used interchangeably, they serve different purposes and function differently.

Mission answers the enduring question: *Why do we exist?*

A church's mission embodies its fundamental identity and purpose. For many churches, this is based on the Great Commission and articulated through continual worship, discipleship, evangelism, and service. Although the wording describing the mission may evolve over time, its core remains largely unchanged.

Vision answers a different kind of question: *What is God calling us to focus on right now?*

Vision is both directional and seasonal, guiding a church to focus its energy and resources on specific goals during a particular phase of ministry. A vision initiative might include launching a new ministry, enhancing discipleship programs, expanding community outreach, or undertaking a building project that supports the church's mission.

Mission anchors the church's identity. Vision mobilizes the church's efforts.

Governance protects the relationship between the two.

Without governance clarity, vision initiatives can quietly reshape a church's identity. New priorities may emerge without careful reflection. Resources may shift in ways that unintentionally redefine what the church values most. Over time, what began as a temporary initiative can slowly become the church's defining focus.

Healthy governance helps prevent this kind of drift. It provides a framework that ensures vision initiatives remain connected to the church's mission and are pursued with transparency and shared understanding.

When leadership operates within clear governance structures, vision can move forward with confidence rather than confusion. Church leaders are free to pursue new opportunities while the church's foundational commitments remain secure.

Mission defines who the church is. Vision clarifies where the church is going. Governance ensures the church moves there faithfully. When these three keep aligned, the church can move forward faithfully without losing sight of who it is and why it exists.

Establishing Review Rhythms

Healthy churches do not wait for conflict to evaluate their governance. They revisit it intentionally. Governance systems naturally drift over time as leadership transitions occur, ministries evolve, and the practical realities of church life change. Documents that once reflected how a church operated can gradually become disconnected from daily practice. When that happens, leaders may begin relying on memory, informal expectations, or personal judgment rather than the structures the church originally established.

Regular review helps prevent that drift. Healthy churches periodically revisit their governance documents to ensure they still reflect how the church actually functions. These reviews do not need to be complicated or disruptive. In many cases, simple rhythms of reflection are enough to maintain clarity. Periodic bylaw reviews allow leaders to identify language that no longer reflects current leadership structures or ministry practices. Annual policy checks provide an opportunity to confirm that expectations remain clear and that procedures continue to support those policies effectively. Leadership training conversations also create space to discuss how governance works in real ministry situations and to address questions before confusion develops.

These rhythms convey something vital to the congregation. They show that governance is not just about storing documents for legal reasons but about a dynamic framework that supports the church's faithful and transparent operation. Churches that ignore these rhythms tend to revisit governance only when issues surface, such as leadership conflicts, policy gaps, or difficult decisions that expose unclear authority. Addressing structural problems during periods of tension is much harder than during stable periods.

Governance health is sustained not by reacting to crises but by ongoing focus. One practical way to maintain that focus is to establish regular habits, such as scheduling recurring governance check-ins on the church calendar. Leadership teams might designate a specific month each year to review bylaws and major policies, or set aside short quarterly agenda items to discuss how governance is working in practice. Reminders about these check-ins can be included in leadership calendars or meeting planners to ensure they are not overlooked amid daily ministry demands. These intentional routines help keep governance on the radar, so it remains a consistent priority rather than fading into the background.

Churches that consistently follow these practices cultivate a culture of clarity over time. Leaders are clear about where to seek guidance, members understand the decision-making process, and expectations remain stable as ministries expand and leadership shifts.

Conclusion

Paul's instruction to the Corinthian church reminds us that the life of the church should reflect the character of God. When he concludes that all things should be done "decently and in order," he addresses the conduct of the gathered church and calls believers to practices that reflect the God of peace rather than confusion.

Order in the church is not about control. It is about creating an environment in which the work of God among his people can flourish without unnecessary disorder or distraction. Paul's concern was that the life of the church should reflect the character of the God they worship.

Similarly, effective governance today enables churches to pursue their mission with clarity and unity. When leaders regularly teach, enforce, and evaluate the structures that shape the church's operations, governance transforms into an integral part of the church's culture rather than being used only during crises.

Over time, this kind of steady attention builds trust. Leaders know how decisions are made. Members understand how they can participate and raise concerns. The church moves forward with confidence because expectations are clear.

Governance reaches maturity not just when documents are written, but when clarity becomes second nature and leaders instinctively follow shared expectations.

Reflection Questions

1. When decisions are made in our church, do leaders naturally reference our governing documents, or do we rely more on memory and informal practices?
2. How are new staff members, ministry leaders, and volunteers introduced to our church's governance structures?
3. Are members of our congregation given clear opportunities to understand how decisions are made and how authority functions within the church?

4. Do we have regular rhythms for reviewing bylaws, policies, or governance practices, or do we tend to revisit them only when problems arise?
5. What one step could our leadership team take this year to strengthen clarity in our church's governance?

CHAPTER 11

STEWARDING RISK - LEGAL, INSURANCE, AND EMERGENCIES

"A well thought-out risk-management plan allows leaders to respond wisely rather than react foolishly to incidents as they occur." Dr. Jody Dean[20]

Most church leaders did not enter ministry expecting to manage insurance, legal obligations, or emergency plans. Seminaries train pastors to preach, shepherd, and lead ministries, but few leaders receive adequate preparation for the practical risks that accompany leading an organization. Yet these responsibilities are part of faithful stewardship. Facilities must be maintained, finances must be protected, and people must be served in ways that safeguard their well-being.

Ignoring these responsibilities does not make them go away. It simply leaves the church unprepared when challenges arise.

Every church has responsibilities beyond Sunday worship. They must maintain facilities, safeguard finances, and serve people in ways that ensure their well-being. Ignoring these responsibilities does not make them go away; it only leaves the church unready to face challenges.

As a result, many churches tend to address these issues only when they become unavoidable. For example, a church may establish a child protection policy only after allegations of misconduct bring deficiencies to light, or reassess insurance coverage when a property incident reveals inadequate protection. Similarly, emergency procedures are often discussed only after a crisis, such as a medical emergency during a service, which forces leadership to confront the need for a structured response.

In other cases, the issue is not a lack of training but a lack of attention. These areas can feel administrative and distant from the visible work of ministry, making them easy to postpone in favor of more immediate priorities. Yet delaying these responsibilities does not reduce the risks a church faces. It simply ensures that preparation happens under pressure rather than with wisdom and foresight.

Wise stewardship recognizes that caring for a congregation includes preparing for challenges leaders hope will never occur. Legal clarity, responsible insurance coverage, and thoughtful emergency planning are not signs of fear or distrust in God's provision. They are practical expressions of pastoral care and responsible leadership.

When churches proactively address these issues before a crisis arises, leaders can focus more fully on their ministry responsibilities, knowing that essential safeguards are in place for unforeseen challenges. By establishing effective governance structures, churches reduce distractions and uncertainty, allowing leaders to dedicate their attention and energy to core ministry tasks. The clarity and stability provided by strong governance, therefore, directly support the church's ability to fulfill its mission with greater assurance.

Why Legal Counsel Matters

Many churches hesitate to seek legal counsel until an issue arises. Pastors and church leaders often assume that attorneys are needed only during conflicts, lawsuits, or major disputes. In reality, the most valuable legal guidance is usually provided long before a crisis ever occurs.

Good legal counsel acts as a form of preventive wisdom.

Attorneys familiar with nonprofit and religious organizations can help churches review governing documents, clarify employment practices, assess liability risks, and ensure policies comply with the law. These discussions can prevent minor oversights from escalating into significant issues. Church leaders seeking qualified legal counsel can often start by asking for referrals from their denominational office, local ministerial networks, or other churches in the community with experience in similar legal matters.

Legal counsel can support churches in many areas. They often seek legal review when creating or updating governing documents, handling employment issues, assessing property transactions, addressing liability concerns, or managing complex situations involving staff, members, or facilities. Since churches function within both a spiritual mission and legal boundaries, careful legal advice helps ensure that ministry decisions are backed by solid organizational practices.

Seeking legal guidance should not be seen as surrendering spiritual leadership to legal authority. The role of an attorney is not to run the church or dictate ministry decisions. Rather, legal counsel helps leaders understand how civil law intersects with the church's governance structures and policies. When those boundaries are understood, leaders are better equipped to lead with confidence.

In many cases, churches only discover gaps in their governance when they are forced to respond quickly to an unexpected situation. A disagreement over employment decisions, a question about member discipline, or a misunderstanding related to facility use can quickly become complicated when governing documents or policies are unclear. Thoughtful legal review helps ensure that the church's structures support its ministry rather than unintentionally exposing it to unnecessary risk.

Wise leaders understand that seeking counsel is not a sign of weakness but a sign of good stewardship. Just as churches depend on accountants for financial guidance and insurance professionals for risk management, legal counsel adds another layer of wisdom that helps maintain the church's long-term health.

When legal counsel is viewed as a resource rather than a last resort, it becomes another tool that helps protect the mission of the church.

Insurance as Ministry Stewardship

Insurance can feel like an administrative burden rather than a ministry priority. Policies, premiums, and coverage limits rarely appear in sermons or ministry reports. Yet insurance plays a significant role in protecting the church's ability to serve its community faithfully.

Churches manage their buildings, vehicles, financial assets, and most importantly, their people. Insurance is in place to safeguard these resources against unforeseen events.

Proper insurance coverage helps protect the church from financial loss caused by accidents, property damage, injuries, or other unforeseen events. More importantly, it safeguards the individuals involved. For instance, if a church van were involved in an accident while transporting youth to an event, appropriate auto and liability insurance would enable the church to care for those affected and cover medical expenses, rather than facing the prospect of canceling future programs or reducing ministry support due to financial hardship. When the right coverage is in place, the church can respond responsibly and compassionately instead of being forced into difficult choices because of financial constraints.

Church leaders should periodically review coverage with professionals who understand the risks churches face. Ministry activities often involve volunteers, large gatherings, children and student programs, transportation, counseling, and community events. Each of these areas carries responsibilities that require thoughtful coverage.

Insurance is not a replacement for trust in God. Scripture never discourages wise preparation. Instead, responsible stewardship recognizes that God entrusts churches with people and resources that deserve careful protection.

When insurance coverage is appropriate and regularly reviewed, leaders gain a measure of freedom. They can pursue ministry opportunities with greater confidence, knowing that reasonable precautions have been taken to protect the church and those it serves.

Insurance does not remove risk, but it enables churches to respond effectively when challenges occur.

Governance in Crisis

Every church will eventually face situations that challenge its leadership. These can include financial difficulties, misconduct allegations, natural disasters, leadership mistakes, or unexpected changes in ministry. When such events happen, the church's governance shifts from a theoretical framework to an immediate practical response.

Crises rarely create governance problems. More often, they reveal them.

When authority is ambiguous, policies are outdated, or leadership roles are not well-defined, a crisis can quickly deepen confusion. Leaders might disagree on who should take action. Decision-making may be slowed by unclear processes. Members could lose confidence in leadership if responses seem inconsistent or makeshift.

Clear governance structures provide stability during these moments.

When roles are defined, policies are established, and leaders understand how decisions are made, the church is better equipped to respond calmly and responsibly. Governance does not remove the emotional weight of difficult situations, but it provides a framework that helps leaders navigate those moments with greater clarity.

Preparation is crucial for handling tough times. Churches that openly discuss potential crisis situations tend to be better prepared to respond effectively in real emergencies. For example, consider a church that faced an unexpected flood requiring immediate evacuation during a weekend service. Because they had established and regularly reviewed emergency procedures, leaders were able to direct volunteers, communicate quickly with families, and coordinate with first responders. The clear policies enabled the church to ensure everyone's safety and continue caring for their members in the aftermath, avoiding confusion or panic. Having clear policies for financial oversight, child protection, staff accountability, and emergency procedures provides important guidance, enabling leaders to face uncertain circumstances with confidence.

During crises, leaders must make decisions that protect people, uphold integrity, and safeguard the church's witness. Governance structures ensure that these decisions are made within an established framework agreed upon by the church.

Healthy governance does not eliminate difficult moments. It simply ensures that when those moments arrive, the church is prepared to respond with wisdom rather than confusion.

When Documents Protect the Church

Governance documents, especially those related to child protection, financial accountability, facility use, and conflict resolution, often seem burdensome until the unfortunate day they become necessary. When the ministry is running smoothly and relationships are strong, these written policies may seem overly cautious or even unnecessary. Leaders may wonder whether detailed documentation is really needed when everyone involved is acting in good faith.

Yet, the times when policies seem unnecessary are often the moments they offer the most protection.

Governance documents are essential for maintaining clarity during stressful situations. When faced with accusations, financial issues, or difficult leadership decisions, the church benefits from clear, pre-existing expectations. Policies enable leaders to respond consistently rather than improvising. They provide a common framework that ensures decisions are grounded in established principles, not temporary feelings.

This kind of clarity protects more than the church as an institution. It protects people. Child protection policies safeguard vulnerable individuals. Financial accountability procedures protect both the church's resources and the leaders entrusted with stewardship. Facility use policies help prevent misunderstandings when church property is shared with others. Conflict resolution processes help leaders navigate disagreements while preserving unity and integrity.

Without these structures, leaders are often forced to make difficult decisions without guidance. In those situations, even well-intentioned responses can appear inconsistent or unfair. Written policies help remove that uncertainty by establishing expectations long before a problem arises.

Wise churches recognize the importance of preparing for unforeseen challenges, understanding that such preparation reflects stewardship rather than pessimism. Careful development and regular review of policies serve as unobtrusive safeguards, allowing the church to advance its mission with greater confidence.

Conclusion

Ministry always carries some measure of risk, making effective stewardship of legal, insurance, and emergency responsibilities a crucial aspect of church leadership. Churches are places where people gather, and wherever crowds assemble, unexpected challenges can arise. Accidents happen, misunderstandings can arise, and unforeseen situations may emerge that leaders never anticipated. Such occurrences do not signify failure but underscore both the complexity of ministry and the essential role of proactive organizational risk management in faithfully stewarding the church's mission.

Wise leaders know that intentional preparation is part of faithful stewardship.

Legal counsel, appropriate insurance coverage, and thoughtful governance policies do not replace prayer, wisdom, or reliance on the Lord. Instead, they support these commitments by enabling the church to respond responsibly when difficult situations arise. When these structures are in place, leaders can focus on the church's mission rather than rushing to address a crisis. Preparation sends an important message to the congregation, demonstrating that leadership is dedicated to caring for people, protecting the church's resources, and upholding integrity in all areas of ministry.

In many ways, good governance quietly protects the church long before problems arise. It sets expectations, clarifies authority, and offers guidance when emotions and pressure might otherwise cloud judgment. Wise church leaders prepare for challenges not out of fear of the worst, but to faithfully steward what God has entrusted to them.

Reflection Questions

1. If our church faced a significant crisis tomorrow, would our current governance structures provide clear guidance for how leaders should respond?

2. When was the last time our leadership team reviewed policies related to child protection, financial accountability, or facility use?
3. Do our leaders know when it is appropriate to seek legal counsel or professional guidance for complex situations?
4. Have we intentionally reviewed our church's insurance coverage to ensure it reflects the realities of our current ministries and activities?
5. In what areas might our church be relying on assumptions or informal practices rather than clear policies?
6. What is one step our leadership team could take this year to strengthen our church's preparedness for unexpected challenges?

CHAPTER 12

GOVERNANCE THAT OUTLASTS ITS LEADERS

Churches often make governance decisions in response to immediate needs. Leaders address current challenges, respond to pressing questions, and work within the personalities of those presently serving. Yet the church is not meant to be built around one leader, one team, or one season. It is part of God's ongoing work across generations.

Psalm 145:4 reminds us of this broader perspective: "One generation shall commend your works to another and shall declare your mighty acts." John Maxwell captures a similar principle when he writes, "A leader's lasting value is measured by succession."[21] The mission of the church is not entrusted to one pastor, leadership team, or season. It is carried forward by generations of believers who build upon the faithfulness of those who came before them. Good governance is vital for keeping this connection strong. It helps ensure that the church's identity, mission, and leadership stay clear and steady, even as pastors transition and new leaders step in.

This final chapter examines how governance helps churches maintain stability during leadership transitions and prepare future generations to lead wisely.

The Myth of Personality-Driven Churches

Many churches go through seasons of health thanks to strong leadership. A talented pastor, a respected lay leader, or a small group of committed individuals can effectively guide the church for many years. During these times, the church often operates smoothly, and formal governance structures may not receive much attention.

The difficulty arises when those leaders move on.

Churches built primarily around personalities often struggle during leadership transitions. Decisions once made informally suddenly become unclear. Expectations long held by leaders are no longer shared by those stepping into new roles. Without clear structures, the church can find itself trying to reconstruct how decisions should be made at the very moment stability is needed most.

Wise churches think about transition before transition arrives. Leadership changes will eventually come, and when they do, the church should not have to depend only on memory, personality, or informal habits. Clear governance helps preserve what leaders have learned, clarify who carries responsibility, and provide guidance for those who will serve next. When important processes are documented and expectations are understood, future leaders can step into their roles with greater confidence and less confusion. This kind of preparation does not remove the emotion of transition, but it helps keep transition from becoming unnecessarily disorienting.

Healthy churches appreciate strong leadership, but they do not depend on personalities alone. Governance structures help ensure that the church's life and mission are not tied to a single individual. When leadership transitions occur, clear governance provides continuity, allowing the church to move forward with confidence rather than uncertainty. Strong leaders serve the church well. Wise governance ensures the church continues to function well after those leaders move on.

Governance as Institutional Memory

One of the most important roles governance plays is serving as the church's institutional memory.

Over the years, churches can build a rich history of traditions, decisions, and shared commitments that shape the congregation's sense of mission. When these meaningful experiences are not documented, that wisdom often remains only in the memories of long-standing members and leaders.

When important decisions live only in the memories of long-time leaders, future leaders are left to guess why certain practices exist. Clear governance preserves that wisdom so each transition does not require the church to start over.

Governance documents help preserve that memory. Constitutions, bylaws, policies, and procedures capture decisions about authority, structure, and expectations that guide the church's life together. These documents remind the congregation who they are, how decisions are made, and what commitments shape their ministry.

Without this kind of institutional memory, each leadership transition risks starting from scratch. New leaders may unintentionally repeat past mistakes or struggle to understand why certain structures exist. Clear governance helps preserve the lessons learned by previous generations of leaders.

In this sense, governance is more than just administration. It is a way to honor the stewardship of those who came before and to guide those who will lead in the future.

Preparing the Next Generation of Leaders

Churches that remain healthy over time are intentional about preparing their future leaders. They recognize that understanding the church's governance structures does not come automatically and is often overlooked.

This gap is understandable. Churches naturally prioritize spiritual development, ministry skills, and immediate practical needs. As a result, governance training is often treated as secondary or assumed rather than taught. In many cases, this gap begins even before ministry starts, as governance receives limited attention in formal ministry training. Yet churches that give attention to this area recognize its importance and intentionally guide emerging leaders in understanding how the church functions.

Leadership development rightly emphasizes spiritual maturity, ministry skills, and theological understanding. These priorities are essential. At the same time, emerging leaders benefit from learning how decisions are made, how authority is shared, and how accountability is practiced within the church. When these areas are understood, leaders are better equipped to serve with wisdom and humility.

Intentional preparation can take many forms. Pastors and experienced leaders can guide emerging leaders through governing documents and explain how they are applied in real-world situations. Leadership meetings can occasionally include discussions on how governance supports ministry decisions. Mentoring relationships offer natural opportunities to explain the reasoning behind policies and structures that might otherwise seem unclear.

Churches may also use more structured approaches, such as onboarding sessions for new leaders, governance workshops, or periodic retreats focused on leadership roles. Practical experiences can be especially helpful. Working through real scenarios, reviewing past decisions, or hearing from experienced leaders can help emerging leaders build both understanding and confidence.

This kind of preparation ensures that future leaders do not inherit governance structures they do not understand. Instead, they step into leadership with clarity about how the church functions and why those systems exist.

Healthy governance is sustained not only by documents but also by leaders who understand, respect, and use them wisely.

Governance as an Act of Love

Governance discussions are sometimes framed in terms of authority, structure, or control. In reality, healthy governance is far more closely connected to care. At its best, governance is an expression of love for God, for the people of the church, and for the mission entrusted to the congregation.

Scripture repeatedly reminds leaders that the church ultimately belongs to the Lord. Throughout the Bible, we see God call His people to steward what has been entrusted to them. For instance, in Numbers 27:15–23, as Moses prepared for his departure, he sought a successor so the community would not be "like sheep without a shepherd." God directed him to appoint Joshua, commissioning him before the congregation and ensuring an orderly, faithful transition of leadership. Similarly, in 1 Chronicles 28–29, King David prepared detailed plans and instructions for building the temple, passing responsibility to Solomon along with encouragement and clear guidelines for governing the work. These stories highlight the importance of stewardship, intentional leadership transitions, and carefully structured guidance that honors God and protects His people.

Stewarding the structures that guide the church's life together is one way leaders demonstrate their love for God and their care for His people. When pastors and church leaders love God deeply, they naturally desire to steward His church well. Loving people means more than preaching faithfully and providing pastoral care. It also means creating structures that protect the congregation from confusion, unfairness, and unnecessary conflict.

When authority is clearly defined, and policies provide guidance, leaders are not forced to improvise difficult decisions under pressure. Members can trust that situations will be handled fairly and transparently. Disagreements are less likely to become personal because the decision-making process is already understood. In these ways, governance quietly protects relationships within the church.

Healthy governance also protects leaders. Pastors and ministry leaders often carry heavy responsibilities, and unclear expectations can place unnecessary strain on those who serve. When governance structures clarify responsibilities and decision-making authority, leaders can serve with greater confidence and less emotional pressure.

Most importantly, good governance allows the church to focus its energy on the mission God has given it. When authority is clear and expectations are shared, leaders spend less time resolving preventable misunderstandings and more time investing in discipleship, ministry, and outreach.

Seen in this light, governance is not about protecting authority. It is about protecting people and faithfully stewarding the church that belongs to God.

Conclusion

Most churches do not prioritize governance until a significant problem makes its importance clear. Challenges such as ambiguous authority in decision-making, uncertainty during leadership transitions, or conflicts that expose deficiencies in policies often reveal the need for strong governance structures. These situations underscore the central lesson of this chapter: proactive and thoughtful governance is essential for ensuring stability, clarity, and faithful continuity within the church, especially during times of change.

Healthy churches choose a different path.

They invest in clarity before confusion arises. They develop structures that support leadership rather than complicate it. They prepare future leaders to understand the systems that guide the church's life together.

The goal of governance is not flawless documents. No set of policies or bylaws can anticipate every issue a church will face. The goal is a community of believers who can move forward together with trust, clarity, and a shared commitment to God's mission.

When governance is healthy, it quietly supports the church's ministry across generations. Leaders may change, but the mission remains steady. Structures provide continuity. Expectations remain clear. The church continues its work faithfully, building on the wisdom and stewardship of those who came before.

In the end, governance is not about managing an organization. It is about stewarding the church that belongs to Christ so that the mission of the gospel continues faithfully from one generation to the next.

Reflection Questions and Actions

1. If a major leadership transition occurred in our church tomorrow, would our governance structures provide clear guidance for how the church should function?
2. In what ways does our church rely on the knowledge or memory of long-time leaders rather than clearly documented governance practices?
3. How are emerging leaders in our church being introduced to the governance structures that guide decision-making?
4. Do our governing documents reflect the lessons and wisdom gained through the church's history?
5. What steps could our leadership take to ensure that future leaders understand both the mission of the church and the governance structures that support it?

PART IV
APPENDIX

APPENDIX A

CHURCH GOVERNANCE ASSESSMENT TOOL

How to Use This Tool

This assessment is designed to help church leaders evaluate how well their current governance supports clarity, trust, and effective ministry.

This is not a test to pass. It is a tool to help you identify your strengths, recognize areas of confusion or risk, and start conversations that lead to greater clarity.

Each statement should be evaluated using the following scale:

1 – Not in place or unclear
2 – Inconsistent or rarely followed
3 – Generally present but needs improvement
4 – Clear and consistently practiced
5 – Clearly defined, consistently practiced, and well understood

Section 1: Constitution (Foundational Clarity)

________ Our church has clearly defined its purpose in a way that remains stable over time
________ Our doctrinal commitments are clearly stated and

understood
________ Our constitution reflects what should remain consistent, not operational details
________ The relationship between our constitution and other governing documents is clear
________ Our amendment process protects important commitments without preventing needed change

Section Score: _______ / 25

Section 2: Bylaws (Authority and Structure)

________ Our bylaws clearly define where decision-making authority rests
________ Leadership roles and responsibilities are clearly described
________ Our bylaws reflect how the church actually functions today
________ Members and leaders know where to look when questions arise
________ Our bylaws avoid unnecessary detail and remain understandable

Section Score: _______ / 25

Section 3: Policies (Consistency and Protection)

________ Our most important policies are written and accessible
________ We have clear personnel and financial policies that are consistently followed
________ We have appropriate safety policies, especially for children and students
________ Policies are applied consistently rather than based on personalities
________ Policies reflect our current ministry practices

Section Score: ______ / 25

Section 4: Procedures (From Policy to Practice)

________ Clear procedures exist for implementing key policies
________ Staff and volunteers understand how to carry out expectations
________ Procedures reflect how ministry actually happens in our church
________ Responsibilities for procedures are clearly assigned
________ Procedures allow for appropriate flexibility when needed

Section Score: ______ / 25

Section 5: Authority and Decision-Making Clarity

________ Leaders can clearly explain who makes decisions in common situations
________ Similar decisions are handled consistently across the church
________ Decision-making processes are understood by both staff and members
________ Authority is not dependent on personalities or informal influence
________ Major decisions follow a clear and trusted process

Section Score: ______ / 25

Section 6: Alignment Between Documents and Practice

________ Our governing documents reflect how the church actually operates

________ We regularly consult our governing documents when making decisions
________ Leaders consistently follow the processes outlined in our documents
________ We are not relying primarily on memory or tradition to guide decisions
________ Outdated practices have been addressed rather than ignored

Section Score: _______ / 25

Section 7: Shadow Governance (Informal Authority)

________ Decision-making authority is clearly defined, not assumed
________ Informal influence does not override formal structures
________ Trusted individuals operate within clearly defined authority
________ We rarely rely on unwritten expectations to guide decisions
________ Leadership decisions are transparent and understandable

Section Score: _______ / 25

Section 8: Readiness for Change and Revitalization

________ Our governance structure supports making difficult decisions when needed
________ Leaders have the authority needed to lead effectively
________ Members trust the process by which decisions are made
________ Governance does not prevent necessary ministry changes

_______ Our church could respond with clarity in a season of transition

Section Score: ______ / 25

Overall Score

Total Score: ______ / 200

Interpreting Your Results

160–200 - Strong clarity and alignment. Governance is likely supporting the ministry effectively.

120–159 - Generally healthy, with some areas that may benefit from refinement.

80–119 - Noticeable gaps in clarity or consistency. Governance may be creating unnecessary strain.

Below 80 - Significant opportunities for improvement. Governance is likely contributing to confusion or limiting effectiveness.

Reflection and Next Steps

Which sections scored the lowest?

Where does your church experience the most confusion or repeated questions?

Are there areas where informal influence is carrying more weight than defined authority?

If your church needed to make a difficult decision tomorrow, where would clarity be lacking?

What is one area of governance that, if improved, would most increase trust and reduce confusion?

A Final Encouragement

Governance often operates quietly in the background, yet it shapes how decisions are made, how leaders lead, and how people experience trust within the church.

This assessment is not about identifying failure. It is about pursuing clarity.

Clear governance reduces anxiety, strengthens trust, and creates space for the church's mission to move forward with confidence.

APPENDIX B

SAMPLE CHURCH CONSTITUTION

Important Notice for Churches:

This sample provides a starting point for discussion and development, not a finalized document. Each church should tailor its governance to fit its specific context, laws, and ministry requirements. Churches are advised to carefully review all governing documents, confirm consistency with their Articles of Incorporation and Bylaws, and seek advice from qualified legal counsel in their state before adopting any governing documents. This sample aims to promote clarity and understanding, but it should not replace thoughtful leadership or professional legal guidance.

This sample Constitution was tailored for a Southern Baptist church.

Preamble

We, the members of [Church Name], believing that the church belongs to Jesus Christ and exists for God's glory, hereby establish this Constitution to guide our life together as a local congregation.

This Constitution is intended to clarify our identity, affirm our shared faith, define our basic structure, and support the mission Christ has entrusted to His church. We seek to order our ministry to reflect biblical faithfulness, congregational unity, responsible stewardship, and commitment to the Great Commission.

Recognizing our dependence on the grace of God and the leadership of the Holy Spirit, we adopt this Constitution as a framework for worship, discipleship, fellowship, service, and mission, so that [Church Name] may faithfully proclaim the gospel, make disciples, and serve our community and the world in the name of Jesus Christ.

Article I: Name

The name of this church shall be
______________________________ ("the Church").

Article II: Purpose

This Church exists to glorify God by making disciples of Jesus Christ.

In keeping with the Great Commission (Matthew 28:18–20), the Church seeks to:

- Proclaim the gospel of Jesus Christ
- Lead people to saving faith in Christ
- Baptize believers
- Teach obedience to all that Christ has commanded
- Equip believers for ministry and mission

Article III: Statement of Faith

This Church affirms the Holy Bible as the inspired, inerrant, and authoritative Word of God and the foundation for all doctrine, belief, and practice.

This Church adopts and affirms the **Baptist Faith and Message (2000)** as a faithful summary of biblical teaching.

While this confession serves as a guiding statement of belief, the Scriptures themselves remain the final authority.

Article IV: Nature and Polity

Section 1. Lordship of Christ

The Lord Jesus Christ is the head of the Church. All authority exercised within the Church is under His lordship.

Section 2. Congregational Governance

The government of this Church is vested in its members. The membership retains the final authority in matters of doctrine, leadership affirmation, and major decisions, consistent with Scripture.

Section 3. Autonomy

This Church is autonomous and not subject to the control of any other ecclesiastical body.

At the same time, the Church recognizes the value of cooperation and voluntarily affiliates with:

- ______________________ Baptist Association
- ______________________ State Convention
- The Southern Baptist Convention

Article V: Membership (Foundational Statement)

The Church is composed of individuals who:

- Have professed faith in Jesus Christ as Lord and Savior
- Have been baptized by immersion as believers
- Commit to live in covenant with the body of Christ

Further details regarding membership processes and responsibilities shall be defined in the Bylaws.

Article VI: Ordinances

The Church recognizes two ordinances given by Christ:

- **Believer's Baptism by immersion**
- **The Lord's Supper**

These ordinances are acts of obedience and symbols of the gospel, not means of salvation.

Article VII: Authority of Governing Documents

This Constitution provides foundational clarity for the Church's identity, doctrine, and authority structure.

The Church's governing documents shall function in the following order:

1. Articles of Incorporation
2. Constitution
3. Bylaws
4. Policies
5. Procedures

No subordinate document may conflict with this Constitution.

Article VIII: Nonprofit Status and Dissolution

This Church is organized exclusively for religious, charitable, and educational purposes consistent with Section 501(c)(3) of the Internal Revenue Code.

In the event of dissolution, the assets of the Church shall be distributed to one or more organizations that:

- Qualify as tax-exempt under Section 501(c)(3), and
- Align with the Church's doctrinal commitments and mission

No part of the assets shall inure to the benefit of any individual.

Article IX: Amendments

This Constitution may be amended by the Church, provided that:

- The proposed amendment is presented in writing at a prior business meeting
- Adequate time is given for review and discussion
- A two-thirds (2/3) vote (or greater, as determined by the Church) is required for approval

Amendments should be approached carefully, recognizing that this document is intended to provide long-term stability.

APPENDIX C

SAMPLE BYLAWS TEMPLATE

Important Notice for Churches:

This sample provides a starting point for discussion and development, not a finalized document. Each church should tailor its governance to fit its specific context, laws, and ministry requirements. Churches are advised to carefully review all governing documents, confirm consistency with their Articles of Incorporation and Bylaws, and seek advice from qualified legal counsel in their state before adopting any governing documents. This sample aims to promote clarity and understanding, but it should not replace thoughtful leadership or professional legal guidance.

These sample bylaws were tailored for a Southern Baptist church.

Article I: Membership

Section 1. Qualifications

Membership in this Church shall consist of individuals who:

- Have professed faith in Jesus Christ as Lord and Savior
- Have been baptized by immersion as believers
- Affirm the Church's statement of faith
- Commit to live in fellowship and accountability within the body

Section 2. Reception of Members

Candidates for membership may be received by:

- Profession of faith and baptism
- Transfer of letter from another church of like faith
- Statement of prior conversion and baptism

Final approval shall be by the Church, as defined by its established process.

Section 3. Responsibilities of Members

Members are expected to:

- Participate in worship and discipleship
- Support the mission of the Church through service and giving
- Pursue unity and spiritual growth

Section 4. Rights of Members

Members in good standing shall have the right to:

- Vote on matters presented to the Church
- Participate in Church meetings
- Be considered for leadership roles, as appropriate

Section 5. Termination of Membership

Membership may be concluded by:

- Transfer to another church
- Request of the member
- Death

- Church discipline, carried out in a biblical and restorative manner

Article II: Church Meetings

Section 1. Worship Gatherings

The Church shall meet regularly for worship, teaching, and fellowship.

Section 2. Business Meetings

Regular and special business meetings may be called as needed.

Section 3. Quorum

A quorum shall consist of those members present at a properly called meeting, unless otherwise defined by the Church.

Section 4. Voting

- Each member in good standing shall have one vote
- Voting thresholds (simple majority, 2/3, etc.) should be clearly defined for key decisions

Article III: Church Governance

Section 1. Authority

Under the lordship of Christ, final earthly authority rests with the congregation.

Section 2. Leadership Structure

The Church shall recognize the following leadership roles (as applicable to its context):

- Pastors/Elders
- Deacons
- Ministry Staff

Section 3. Delegation of Authority

The Church may delegate specific responsibilities to leaders, staff, and committees, while retaining final authority as defined in the Constitution.

Article IV: Pastoral Leadership

Section 1. Role of the Pastor

The Pastor(s) shall:

- Provide spiritual leadership
- Preach and teach the Word of God
- Lead the Church in fulfilling its mission
- Oversee staff and ministry direction (as defined by the Church)

Section 2. Selection of Pastor

The process for selecting a Pastor shall include:

- A search process defined by the Church
- Recommendation to the congregation
- Approval by a defined voting threshold

Section 3. Accountability

The Pastor shall be accountable to the Church, with support and evaluation processes defined appropriately.

Article V: Deacons (or Equivalent Leadership Body)

Section 1. Role

Deacons shall serve the Church by:

- Supporting pastoral leadership
- Assisting in ministry care
- Helping maintain unity within the body

Section 2. Selection

- Nominated and affirmed by the Church
- Meet biblical qualifications (Acts 6, 1 Timothy 3)

Section 3. Responsibilities

Specific responsibilities may be defined by the Church but should not conflict with the overall governance structure.

Article VI: Committees and Ministry Teams

Section 1. Purpose

Committees and teams may be formed to support the ministry and operations of the Church.

Section 2. Authority

Committees serve in an advisory or delegated role and do not hold authority beyond what is granted by the Church.

Article VII: Financial Stewardship

Section 1. Budget

An annual budget shall be prepared and presented to the Church for approval.

Section 2. Oversight

Financial oversight shall include:

- Defined responsibility for handling funds
- Regular reporting to the Church
- Appropriate internal controls

Article VIII: Church Staff

Section 1. Employment

The Church may call or employ staff as needed to support ministry.

Section 2. Supervision

Staff shall be supervised according to the leadership structure established by the Church.

Section 3. Policies

Personnel matters shall be governed by policies adopted by the Church or its designated leadership.

Article IX: Ordinances

The Church shall observe:

- Baptism
- The Lord's Supper

Administration shall be overseen by the Pastor(s) and Church leadership.

Article X: Amendments

These Bylaws may be amended provided that:

- The proposed amendment is presented in writing in advance
- Adequate time is given for review
- Approval is granted by a defined voting threshold

APPENDIX D

SAMPLE POLICY CATEGORIES

Important Notice for Churches:

This sample provides a starting point for discussion and development, not a finalized document. Each church should tailor its governance to fit its specific context, laws, and ministry requirements. Churches are advised to carefully review all governing documents, confirm consistency with their Articles of Incorporation and Bylaws, and seek advice from qualified legal counsel in their state before adopting any governing documents. This sample aims to promote clarity and understanding, but it should not replace thoughtful leadership or professional legal guidance.

Core Policy Categories

The following categories represent critical areas most churches should consider addressing. Not every church will develop all of these at once, but each area reflects common risks, responsibilities, and recurring decision-making.

1. Governance and Authority Policies

These policies clarify how decisions are made within the framework of the church's governing documents.

Examples include:

- Delegation of authority

- Committee and team responsibilities
- Approval thresholds for major decisions
- Decision-making processes

2. Financial Stewardship Policies

These policies provide clarity and accountability in how church resources are handled.

Examples include:

- Budget development and approval
- Spending and approval limits
- Handling of contributions and designated gifts
- Reimbursements and expense policies
- Internal controls and financial reporting
- Audit or financial review practices

3. Personnel and Volunteer Policies

These policies guide how the church cares for and leads those who serve.

Examples include:

- Hiring and onboarding processes
- Employee expectations and conduct
- Compensation and benefits (if applicable)
- Volunteer qualifications and expectations
- Discipline and termination processes

4. Safety and Risk Management Policies

These are among the most important policies a church can develop.

Examples include:

- Child and student protection policies
- Background checks and screening
- Two-adult or supervision guidelines
- Emergency response procedures
- Medical incident response
- Incident reporting

5. Facility and Property Use Policies

These policies clarify how church property is used and protected.

Examples include:

- Facility use approval process
- Outside group usage
- Scheduling and priority of use
- Care and responsibility for property
- Liability and insurance requirements

6. Benevolence and Assistance Policies

These policies guide how the church provides care and financial assistance.

Examples include:

- Eligibility and application process
- Approval authority
- Limits and frequency of assistance
- Documentation and confidentiality

7. Communication and Technology Policies

These policies help protect both the church and individuals in an increasingly digital environment.

Examples include:

- Use of church communication platforms
- Social media guidelines
- Data privacy and information security
- Use of church-owned technology

8. Record Keeping and Documentation Policies

These policies ensure that important information is handled responsibly.

Examples include:

- Financial record retention
- Membership records
- Personnel files
- Confidential information handling

9. Conflict of Interest and Ethics Policies

These policies protect the integrity of leadership and decision-making.

Examples include:

- Disclosure of financial interests
- Related-party transactions
- Ethical conduct expectations

10. Ministry-Specific Policies (As Needed)

As churches grow, additional policies may be needed for specific ministries.

Examples include:

- Preschool or school operations
- Counseling or care ministries
- Transportation and vehicle use
- Missions and trip guidelines

APPENDIX E

10 QUESTIONS TO ASK ABOUT YOUR CHURCH CONSTITUTION

1. Does it clearly identify the church?

A constitution should clearly state the church's official name and basic identity. This helps avoid confusion among legal, ministry, campus, and historical names that may have been used over time.

2. Does it clearly state the church's purpose?

The constitution should explain, in broad, enduring terms, why the church exists. This section should usually be tied to worship, discipleship, fellowship, ministry, evangelism, missions, and the Great Commission rather than to a temporary vision statement.

3. Does it include a clear statement of faith?

A constitution should identify the doctrinal commitments that guide the church's teaching and cooperation. For Baptist churches, this may include adopting or affirming a confession such as the Baptist Faith and Message.

4. Does it define membership at a foundational level?

The constitution should explain who may become a member and what membership means. Detailed membership processes can be placed in the bylaws, but the constitution should make clear that membership is a covenant commitment, not merely attendance.

5. Does it clarify where final authority rests?

In a congregational church, the constitution should clearly define the congregation's role in major decisions. This helps protect both pastoral leadership and congregational responsibility.

6. Does it identify major leadership roles?

The constitution should identify the church's basic leadership offices or roles, such as pastors, deacons, elders, trustees, or other recognized leaders. The details of selection, terms, and responsibilities can be set forth in the bylaws.

7. Does it include a dissolution clause?

The constitution should specify what happens to church assets if the church dissolves. This language should protect the church's charitable and ministry purposes and be reviewed with legal counsel.

8. Is the amendment process careful but not impossible?

A constitution should be harder to amend than policies or procedures because it protects foundational commitments. At the same time, the amendment process should not be so difficult that needed corrections become impossible.

9. Is it short enough to be understood?

A constitution should not try to manage daily ministry decisions. If it is filled with operational details, it may become too difficult to amend and too complicated for members to understand.

10. Does it contradict the Articles of Incorporation or the bylaws?

The constitution should not conflict with the church's Articles of Incorporation or bylaws. If these documents overlap or disagree, the church should seek qualified legal guidance.

11. You probably need a lawyer!

Some issues are important enough to break the numbering. Before making major changes to a constitution, bylaws, or Articles of Incorporation, churches should consult qualified legal counsel. A good church attorney can help identify conflicts, clarify legal concerns, and ensure that the church's governing documents support rather than undermine one another.

This is especially important when changes involve membership, leadership authority, property, dissolution, employment, or denominational relationships. A little legal guidance before a vote can prevent a great deal of confusion after one.

APPENDIX F

10 QUESTIONS TO ASK ABOUT YOUR CHURCH BYLAWS

1. Do they clearly define authority?

Bylaws should answer the question, "Who has authority to make this decision?" They should also clarify the roles of the congregation, pastors, staff, elders, deacons, trustees, committees, and ministry teams.

2. Do they explain how leaders are selected?

The bylaws should clearly outline how pastors, deacons, elders, trustees, officers, or other leaders are nominated, examined, elected, appointed, or affirmed. This is especially important during leadership transitions.

3. Do they explain how leaders can be removed?

Removal processes should be clear, fair, and careful. Churches often avoid this section because it feels uncomfortable, but unclear removal language can lead to major conflict when difficult situations arise.

4. Do they define membership processes?

Bylaws should explain how people become members, how membership is maintained, how members may be removed, and how membership may be restored. This helps the church manage membership consistently and with care.

5. Do they explain church meetings?

Bylaws should clarify regular meetings, special-called meetings, notice requirements, quorum, voting thresholds, and who may vote. These details matter greatly when important decisions are before the church.

6. Do they explain financial authority?

The bylaws should specify who approves the budget, who may authorize major financial decisions, and which decisions require congregational approval. Detailed financial controls may belong in policy, but the authority structure belongs in the bylaws.

7. Do they avoid unnecessary operational detail?

Bylaws should not include every ministry procedure, job description, or workflow. Too much detail makes bylaws difficult to update and increases the risk that the church will unintentionally violate its own rules.

8. Do they align with actual practice?

If the church regularly operates differently from what the bylaws say, either the practice needs to change or the bylaws need to be updated. Bylaws that are ignored lose credibility and create risk.

9. Do they include a clear amendment process?

The bylaws should outline how changes are proposed, communicated, discussed, and approved. Members are more likely to trust changes when the process is transparent and consistently applied.

10. Are they readable for church leaders and members?

Bylaws should be precise, but not so technical that only a lawyer can understand them. A good set of bylaws should be clear enough for leaders to use when making real ministry decisions.

APPENDIX G

10 QUESTIONS TO ASK ABOUT YOUR CHURCH POLICIES

1. Are the most important policies written down?

Many churches have policies that exist only in memory or tradition. Important areas such as finances, personnel, child protection, facility use, benevolence, records, and conflict should be documented and approved.

2. Are they connected to the proper authority?

A policy should clearly state who approved it and who is responsible for carrying it out. Policies should not be disconnected from the church's bylaws or leadership structure.

3. Do they answer "what should happen?"

Policies should establish expectations, boundaries, and permissions. They should not be lost in the details of implementation, which usually belong in procedures.

4. Are they clear enough to apply consistently?

A good policy should help leaders handle similar situations consistently. If the language is vague, leaders may apply it differently, creating confusion and raising questions about fairness.

5. Do they protect people?

Policies should be evaluated by asking, "Who does this protect?" Strong policies protect children, students, vulnerable adults, staff, volunteers, members, guests, leaders, and the church's witness.

6. Do they protect financial integrity?

Financial policies should address spending authority, reimbursements, accounting procedures, restricted gifts, credit cards, audits or reviews, and internal controls. These policies protect both the church and those handling money.

7. Do they reflect current ministry practice?

Policies should align with how the church actually operates. If the church has added ministries, staff, school programs, online giving, livestreaming, or new facility uses, older policies may need revision.

8. Are they accessible to those who need it?

A policy that no one can find will not help the church. Staff, ministry leaders, volunteers, and committee members should know where to access the policies that affect their areas of service.

9. Is there a review schedule?

Policies should be reviewed regularly, especially in areas involving children, finances, personnel, safety, insurance, facilities, and records. Annual or biennial reviews help keep policies current before problems arise.

10. Are they communicated and taught?

Approving a policy is not the same as implementing it. Leaders should explain major policies to those affected so expectations are clear before a difficult situation arises.

APPENDIX H

10 QUESTIONS TO ASK ABOUT YOUR CHURCH PROCEDURES

1. Do they explain "how" clearly?

A procedure should provide practical steps for implementing a policy. If a policy states what should happen, the procedure should explain how it is actually carried out.

2. Is the first step obvious?

A good procedure should make it clear where to begin. If a volunteer, staff member, or ministry leader does not know the first step, the procedure needs to be simplified.

3. Are they written in plain language?

Procedures should be easy to follow. Avoid technical language when simple terms will suffice. The goal is not to impress the reader but to help the church act consistently.

4. Is it assigned to a role?

Procedures should be owned by a role, not just a person. For example, "Facilities Coordinator" is better than "Susan handles this" because people change, but roles provide continuity.

5. Does the procedure match real ministry workflow?

Procedures should reflect how ministry actually happens. If a procedure looks good on paper but does not work on Sunday morning, during a funeral, or at a student event, it needs adjustment.

6. Does it allow appropriate flexibility?

Some procedures must be firm, especially in areas such as safety, child protection, finances, and legal compliance. Other procedures may allow for discernment through phrases such as “typically,” “as appropriate,” or “in consultation with.”

7. Is it easy to find?

A procedure should be stored where the people who use it can access it. If procedures are buried in someone’s email, in old files, or in memory, they will not be followed consistently.

8. Does it include documentation when needed?

Some procedures should create records, such as incident reports, facility use approvals, reimbursement forms, background checks, benevolence requests, or meeting minutes. Documentation helps ensure clarity and accountability.

9. Has it been tested?

A procedure should be tested by the people who will use it. If it is confusing, too long, or unrealistic, revise it before expecting everyone to follow it.

10. Is there a plan to review and update it?

Procedures often need to change more frequently than constitutions, bylaws, or policies. As ministries grow, technology evolves, staff roles shift, or problems arise, procedures should be adjusted to remain useful.

APPENDIX I

ADDITIONAL RESOURCES

Thank you for taking the time to read and use this book. My prayer is that it serves you, your leadership team, and your church as you work to build governance that is both faithful and clear.

Because every church is different, no single book can address every question, document, or situation a pastor may face. My hope is to continue developing practical resources that help churches think carefully about governance, leadership, policies, and ministry structure.

For additional resources, updates, sample tools, and ways to contact me, please visit www.bradgwartney.com

There you will find more information about Faithful and Clear, along with resources to help pastors and church leaders apply these principles in their own ministry context.

Thank you again for your commitment to serving the local church with clarity and faithfulness.

NOTES

---

[1] Mark Clifton, *Reclaiming Glory: Revitalizing Dying Churches* (Nashville: B&H Publishing Group, 2016), 68.

[2] Southern Baptist Convention, "*The Baptist Faith and Message 2000*," accessed April 18, 2026, https://bfm.sbc.net.

[3] Adam Harwood, *Christian Theology: Biblical, Historical, and Systematic* (Bellingham, WA: Lexham Press, 2022), 655.

[4] Southern Baptist Convention, "*The Baptist Faith and Message 2000*."

[5] Herschel H. Hobbs, *The Baptist Faith and Message*, rev. ed. (Nashville: Convention Press, 1996), 70.

[6] Stanley J. Grenz, David Guretzki, and Cherith Fee Nordling, *Pocket Dictionary of Theological Terms* (Downers Grove, IL: InterVarsity Press, 1999), 17–18.

[7] Richard R. Hammar, "*Dissolution*," *Church Law & Tax*, accessed April 18, 2026, https://www.churchlawandtax.com/pastor-church-law/organization-and-administration/dissolution/.

[8] "*Church Not Following Bylaws: What You Can Do*," *LegalClarity*, accessed April 18, 2026, https://legalclarity.org/church-not-following-bylaws-what-you-can-do/.

[9] Richard R. Hammar, "'*Neutral Principles' in Church Property Disputes*," *Church Law & Tax Report*, 1996, accessed April 18, 2026, https://www.churchlawandtax.com/legal-developments/neutral-principles-in-church-property-disputes/.

[10] Lynn Buzzard, *Church Policy Manual Guidebook: A Legal and Practical Guide for Developing Church Policies* (Raleigh, NC: Baptist State Convention of North Carolina, 2004), 356.

[11] Robert H. Welch, *Church Administration: Creating Efficiency for Effective Ministry* (Nashville: B&H Academic, 2005), 51.

[12] David W. Duffy, "*What Does Culture Eats Strategy for Breakfast Mean?,*" *The Corporate Governance Institute*, accessed May 2, 2026, https://www.thecorporategovernanceinstitute.com/insights/lexicon/what-does-culture-eats-strategy-for-breakfast-mean/.

[13] Dan Hotchkiss, "*Why Congregations Sometimes Change,*" *Leading Ideas*, 2024, accessed May 2, 2026, https://www.churchleadership.com/leading-ideas/why-congregations-sometimes-change/.

[14] Dean Inserra, *Church, What Is It All About?* (Brentwood, TN: B&H Publishing Group, 2024), 25.

[15] Adam Hughes and Jody Dean, *Together We Lead* (Birmingham, AL: New Hope Publishers, 2021), 125.

[16] Kenneth C. Haugk, *Antagonists in the Church: How to Identify and Deal with Destructive Conflict* (St. Louis, MO: Tebunah Ministries, 2013), 180.

[17] Haugk, *Antagonists in the Church*, 170.

[18] "*The Time to Prepare,*" *The Wooden Effect*, accessed May 2, 2026, https://www.thewoodeneffect.com/the-time-to-prepare/.

[19] Tod E. Bolsinger, *Tempered Resilience: How Leaders Are Formed in the Crucible of Change* (Downers Grove, IL: InterVarsity Press, 2020), 26.

[20] Hughes and Dean, *Together We Lead*, 125.

[21] John C. Maxwell, "*Leaving a Legitimate Legacy,*" *Maxwell Leadership*, July 3, 2013, accessed May 4, 2026, https://www.maxwellleadership.com/blog/leaving-a-legitimate-legacy/.

www.ingramcontent.com/pod-product-compliance
Lightning Source LLC
LaVergne TN
LVHW050640100826
845148LV00011B/1925
* 9 7 9 8 2 3 4 0 8 4 1 3 2 *